Welcome . . . and congratulations!

Congratulations? For what? Well, studies show that the single most important factor in a smooth divorce is starting off with the right information. The fact that you are reading my book shows you have a desire to know and participate that will lead you to successful solutions. You are definitely on the right path.

My life's work has been to develop ways to help people take some control when going through a divorce—one of life's toughest passages. Divorce is hard enough without having to struggle against a legal system that tends to make things worse instead of better. If you follow my advice, you won't have to go through that.

Divorce Helpline. After 30 years of producing materials to help people help themselves, the next step was to reinvent the practice of law. My goal was to develop a way for lawyers to help people in a way that would be effective and affordable; a practice that would solve problems, not cause them. So in 1990, Sherman, Williams & Lober was formed and Divorce Helpline was born. Over time we grew, and in 2007 became Sherman, Naraghi, Woodcock & Pipersky, with more talent and energy than ever, to bring you the best and most effective service in Texas (or anywhere). Texas attorney Bruce Naraghi handles and supervises all Texas cases.

Many people can get through a divorce without any help outside the covers of my books—and well over a million people have done so. The books are as complete as I know how to make them without becoming cumbersome, but books can't replace years of experience. People with some resources to protect will find that doing their own divorce with the help of an experienced Divorce Helpline attorney can save money and bring peace of mind. This is just one more tool we have invented to help you help yourself. You get to choose what works best for you.

This is a book you can talk to. If you have questions to ask or problems to solve, or if you want a friendly, reliable attorney to act as your coach or "just do it" for you, call Divorce Helpline. Tell them Ed Sherman sent you.

Ed Sherman

Doing your own divorce doesn't mean that you can't get help.

The important thing is that you keep control of your own case. We created Divorce Helpline to provide legal support and practical advice for people doing their own divorces. When you use Divorce Helpline, you are still doing your own divorce, because the control of your case and your life stays in your hands, where it belongs.

At Divorce Helpline we are expert at helping you solve problems, settle issues, negotiate agreements, and get through your divorce in the best way possible. We do not take cases to court; instead we use discussion, negotiation, mediation, collaborative divorce and arbitration. Our highly experienced, top-quality attorneys have helped over 60,000 people since 1990, so we can almost certainly help you.

We are friendly, supportive, easy to talk to and easy to reach. Call and ask for more information about how Divorce Helpline can help you.

Video Conference Available

Consult with us in a secure video connection or in a group conference for negotiation or mediation. There is no additional charge for this service.

All you need is a computer, broadband and a webcam.

Call for an appointment and easy setup instructions.

Twelfth Edition
for 2009–2011

Nolo Press Occidental
501 Mission Street, Suite 2
Santa Cruz, CA 95060
(831) 466-9922

DATED MATERIAL

THIS BOOK WAS PRINTED IN

AUGUST 2009

Check with your local bookstore to be sure this is the
most recent printing of the book before you start!

DO NOT USE AN OLD EDITION OF THIS BOOK!

Out-of-date forms and information can cause trouble

30% OFF ON UPDATES

If you have an older edition of this book and want to update, tear off
the cover and send it to us with $20.97 plus $5 shipping = $25.97 total.

FREE UPDATE NOTICES ONLINE

Look for new laws, forms, and fixes at

www.nolodivorce.com/alerts

ISBN13/EAN: 978-0-944508-70-1

Library of Congress Control Number: 2009927695

Printed in U.S.A.

Contents

Part One: All About Divorce

Contents

Part Two: How to Do Your Own Divorce

CD with forms, codes, agreement and more!   **Inside back cover**

Part One:

All About Divorce

This book is dedicated to all of my clients
and to my ex-wife
from whom I have learned so much
about the subject in these pages

Design and graphics: Ed Sherman

A. Doing Your Own Divorce

You might not know it, but you are going through two divorces at the same time—your Real Divorce and your Legal Divorce.

This book is about getting through the legal divorce with minimum involvement with courts and lawyers. It explains Texas divorce laws, with practical advice to help you make decisions, and shows you exactly how to do the paperwork to get your divorce or find someone to do it for you inexpensively.

The real divorce is your life, your relationships with your Ex, family, friends, children, and—most of all—yourself. It's what you go through in practical, emotional, and spiritual terms. The real divorce is about breaking old patterns, finding a new center for your life and doing your best with the hand you've been dealt. These matters are not assisted or addressed in any way by the legal divorce.

The legal divorce cares only about how you will divide marital property and debts, whether there will be spousal support, and how you will arrange parenting and child support if you have minor children. If you can settle these matters out of court, there's nothing left but paperwork and red tape to get your Decree of Divorce.

If you have trouble agreeing on terms, the problem is almost never legal, but almost always about personalities and emotional upset, for which there is absolutely no help and no solutions—zip, zero, nothing—in court or in a lawyer's office. In fact, getting involved with lawyers and courts almost always makes things worse—much worse. If you follow my advice, you'll avoid the traps and pitfalls of the legal system, and things will get much better much sooner.

1. Can you do your own divorce? Should you?

Yes! You can! Since this book was first published in 1980, hundreds of thousands of Texans just like you have used it to do their divorces without retaining lawyers, so you can almost certainly do it, too. This book can save you thousands of dollars!

Yes! You should do your own divorce! Taking charge of your own case leads to a smoother, faster, less painful, and less expensive experience. Most people would be better off if they reduced or eliminated their use of attorneys, because the legal process—and the way attorneys work in it—tends to cause trouble, raise the level of conflict, and greatly increase the cost. While you might decide to get advice from a family law attorney who primarily practices mediation or collaborative law, you should not *retain* an attorney to "take your case" unless you have an unavoidable need for doing so. In section 7 below I explain when you should get help and, in section 8, how to get the right kind of help from an attorney without *retaining* him/her to take over your case.

What if things don't go smoothly—easy and difficult cases. If your spouse will not oppose you in court because he/she is gone, doesn't care, or you expect no trouble agreeing on terms, then you only need some paperwork to get your divorce done, and this is the only book you'll need. However, if you have trouble agreeing on divorce terms (or think you will), or if you prefer to have a professional stand with you and take an active role in negotiating for you, or if your case seems headed for court, you can still do your own divorce, and this book is an important place to start, but you will need more help. Solving divorce problems is discussed below in section 6 and getting the right help is discussed in section 8.

2. What "do your own divorce" means

Doing your own paperwork is not the important thing—the essence of it is thinking things through and making informed decisions. It means that you take responsibility for your case, your decisions, your life. You find out what the rules are and how they apply to your case. You explore all options, then decide what you want and how you want to go about it. If you use an attorney, *you* make all the decisions and control how your case is run. If your spouse is in the picture and cares what happens, doing your own divorce means having detailed discussions—perhaps with help—to reach a thoroughly negotiated agreement.

Above all, doing your own divorce means that you do not *retain* an attorney (more on this below). No one should *retain* an attorney unless they have an emergency situation like those discussed below in section 7, but that doesn't mean you can't get advice and help from an attorney if you feel the need (section 8).

Many people find it difficult to think things through carefully and make decisions about their divorce, and they are *extremely* nervous about discussing divorce details with their Ex. This is completely understandable, but it is something you need to do if you don't want to become a victim of divorce. If you want it, you can get help from an attorney-mediator or a collaborative law attorney (section 8) to help you think things through, talk to your spouse, and work out an agreement.

a) What it means to "retain" an attorney (and why you don't want to)

It's okay to use an attorney, but most people should not *retain* one in their divorce unless there is a clear reason for doing so (see section 7 below). Here's why. When you *retain* an attorney, you sign a "retainer agreement" where the attorney takes responsibility for acting in your behalf—to represent you. You are *literally* handing over your power and authority to act. Standards of professional conduct require any attorney who represents you—even one with good intentions—to act in ways that will complicate your case and make it worse instead of better. Attorneys typically start cases in court quickly, even when that is likely to cause upset and make settlement more difficult.

An attorney who represents you must go to great lengths to protect himself against later malpractice claims by his own client—you. This means doing things for the attorney's benefit instead of yours. Doing the maximum may or may not help you, but it will certainly raise the level of conflict, and it will cost plenty.

Never forget that when you *retain* an attorney, the more trouble you have, the more money the attorney makes. That's hardly an incentive to keep things simple.

Our legal system is known as "the adversary system," which means that attorneys work as combatants, fighting to "win." This is not the best way to go about solving family and personal problems.

It would be nice if you could get help from an experienced attorney with a good attitude who does not want to be retained, but few attorneys will take an interest in your case unless you retain them. That's why we created Divorce Helpline, operated by Sherman, Naraghi, Woodcock & Pipersky. This is the only law firm we know of that works exclusively on divorce settlement. Instead of "taking" your case, we serve as your guide and assistant. When you use Divorce Helpline, you are still doing your own divorce because the responsibility and control of the case stays in your hands. We guide you, help resolve problems, and handle the red tape and paperwork, but your case doesn't get out of control because *you* are in charge.

b) Making decisions

Part of the service you are supposed to get from a lawyer is help with making decisions. Lawyers know what has to be decided and the general standards and rules by which things are done in courts in your community. This is what the first part of this book is all about. It tells you what needs to be decided and how things are done in cases where there is no fight. It gives you information and help with making your own decisions.

If, after reading this book, you can make your own decisions based on your own knowledge, then you probably do not need a lawyer. If you read this book and still have doubts or questions, then you probably should have professional advice. It may be that you can find an attorney who will help you settle your mind, then you can go on to do the rest on your own. Section 8 below tells you how to find such a person.

Things that must be decided

- that the marriage should be ended forever, and
- how to divide any property and bills that you may have accumulated during the marriage, and
- whether there will be alimony and, if so, how much.

If you have no minor children, that's all there is to it. If you do have minor children, you must also decide:

- who is to have custody of the children,
- how care time (visitation) will be arranged, and
- how much is to be paid for support.

As far as the law is concerned, this is what a divorce is all about—settling the practical affairs of the couple and watching out for the well-being of the children. These are the things you must decide about in order to get a divorce. If your spouse is in the picture and cares about what happens in the divorce, then either you must be able to talk things over and agree on these things, or you must be sure that your spouse will not get a lawyer and oppose you legally.

c) Advantages to doing your own divorce

Getting a good divorce

Studies show that active participation in your divorce is the single most important factor in getting a good divorce. "Good divorce" means such things as better compliance with agreements and orders after the divorce, less post-divorce conflict, less post-divorce litigation, more good will, and better co-parenting.

People who take an active role generally do much better emotionally and legally than those who try to avoid the responsibility for solving their divorce problems. This doesn't mean you shouldn't get help from an attorney or mediator—it means you should be actively involved, become informed about the rules, and make your own decisions. Be in charge of your case and your life. Don't be a victim; be a participant in your divorce.

It's much cheaper

A huge advantage to doing your own divorce, even with the help of Divorce Helpline, is the savings in cost. When an attorney takes your case, the initial retainer could be anywhere from $750 to $5,000, but the retainer is only the beginning. The average cost of a divorce is about $20,000 *for each party*, but that's only because the average couple has no more than that to spend. If you have more, it will cost more—much more. Depending on the size of your estate, a contested case can cost many tens or hundreds of thousands of dollars *on each side!*

Keeping it simple

Most people start off with a case that is either fairly simple or that could probably become simple if handled right. Such cases don't usually stay simple after an attorney is retained. Divorces are sensitive, so it doesn't take much to stir them up, but lawyers and the legal system tend to make things more complicated, stirred up, worse instead of better. This is because of the way the system works and the way lawyers work in it.

When one spouse or partner gets an attorney, the other is likely to get one too, and then the fun really begins. Two attorneys start off costing just double, but pretty soon they are writing unpleasant letters, filing motions, and doing attorney-type things as a matter of routine that may not be helpful. Now we have a contested case, more fees and charges, and a couple of very upset and broke spouses.

In the end, you will still have to negotiate a settlement with your Ex. Over 90% of all cases settle without trial, but when attorneys are retained, settlement usually comes after the parties are emotionally depleted and their bank accounts exhausted. Why go through all that?

The moral of this story is this: don't *retain* an attorney unless you absolutely must (section 7 below). If you do it entirely yourself, or with the help of Divorce Helpline, you have a much better chance of keeping a simple case simple and of reaching a settlement much earlier.

3. Divorce basics

a) Grounds for divorce

To get a divorce, you have to have a legally approved reason, known as *grounds*, for your divorce. Uncontested divorces are almost always based on the grounds that the marriage is *insupportable*—that is, it is no one's fault, but the marriage has broken down so badly that it can't be saved. This is called a no-fault divorce and is the most civilized way to go. Unfortunately, Texas law makes it possible for a spouse to get a larger share of the community property by proving that the other spouse was at fault, typically by alleging adultery or cruelty. Attempting a case based on fault will likely lead to lawyers and a long, nasty, and very expensive divorce with an unpredictable outcome. In this book, we assume you will be getting a no-fault divorce.

The grounds of insupportability. You can be divorced if your marriage ". . . has become insupportable because of discord or conflict of personalities that destroys the legitimate ends of the marriage relationship and prevents any reasonable expectation of reconciliation." This probably means that you don't get along in a way that seems both important and permanent. But you can't just say it this way—that would be too easy. Instead, when you go into court you must tell the judge exactly those words quoted above. If you had an attorney, he or she would say the words for you, then ask you, "Isn't that true?" while nodding "Yes." You would then say "Yes," and that would be that. If you can bear the burden of saying these words on your own, then you don't need the attorney. It is, by the way, almost unheard of for a divorce not to be granted because of insufficient grounds.

There are six other grounds for divorce, two of which also involve no fault (living apart for more than three years and confinement in a mental hospital), and four of which involve fault (cruelty, adultery, conviction of a felony, and abandonment). Way over 99% of all cases are run on the grounds of "insupportability." Even if your case falls under one of the other categories, you still call it "insupportability." It's easier and it's the expected thing.

b) Jurisdiction (power of the court)

"Jurisdiction" means the legal right and power to make and enforce orders. In a divorce case, you are asking the court to make orders about your marriage, your property, your kids, and your spouse. The court has power to make orders about matters within the borders of Texas, so if you, your spouse, the kids, and the property are all in Texas, everything is fine. Just show that you satisfy the residency requirement, and you're on your way. But where would a Texas judge get off making orders about a spouse or kids or property if they were in some other state?

If your spouse resides permanently outside of Texas, then the court cannot have personal jurisdiction over your spouse unless your case satisfies the requirements of the "long-arm jurisdiction" rules. As a matter of fact, in many cases, you can get along just fine without having personal jurisdiction over your spouse. This is where there are no children, no property outside of Texas that you want to have, and no need to order your spouse to pay debts. But where there is a child, or important property outside of Texas that you want, or a need to order your spouse to pay debts, then you cannot do your own divorce in Texas unless you satisfy the long-arm rules.

"Long-arm jurisdiction" is, just as it sounds, when the court gets the right to make orders that reach out beyond the borders of Texas. There are actually two long-arm rules—the "marital long-arm" and the "parent/child long-arm."

1) **The marital long-arm.** If your spouse permanently resides outside of Texas, then the court can have personal jurisdiction over your spouse only if Texas is the last state in which you and your spouse had marital cohabitation (lived together as man and wife) and if your divorce suit is started within two years of the last time you cohabited. Even if you cannot satisfy this rule, you can still do your divorce if you do not need an order for the transfer of out-of-state property or for the payment of debts.

2) **The parent/child long-arm.** If there is a child, then you must satisfy this rule. The court can have jurisdiction over your case only if:

   i) your spouse is personally served with Citation while in Texas; *or*

   ii) your spouse consents to jurisdiction in Texas, by appearing in court or filing a document such as the Waiver (chapter 6A); *or*

   iii) the child resides in Texas because of some act of your spouse, or with your spouse's approval; *or*

   iv) your spouse resided in Texas and provided prenatal expenses or support for the child (this is presumed if you and your spouse were living together during the pregnancy); *or*

   v) the child was conceived in Texas.

There may be other ways for the court to get power to act in your case, but you will need an attorney to explore them and to plead them to the court properly.

c) Residency requirements

Residency in Texas is what gives the court power to dissolve your marriage. No matter where you were married—some other state or some other country—if you meet the residency requirement, you can be divorced in Texas.

The residency requirement. In the period immediately before filing your divorce, either you or your spouse must have been a domiciliary (resident) of Texas for at least six months and a resident of the county where you file it for at least 90 days. "Domiciliary" means you have your residence in Texas with the intention to live here permanently. It is okay to be absent on a temporary trip so long as you always intend to return. Also, a person does not lose domiciliary status if absent from the state for military or public service for the state or nation. You are a "resident" of a county simply by living there, no matter what your intentions. Finally, you don't have to stay in Texas or in your county after the divorce is filed; it is okay to move anywhere you like once those papers are stamped by the clerk.

d) Notice to your spouse

A lawsuit is regarded as a struggle between two contestants, conducted before an impartial authority (judge) who decides the matter. It seems obvious (doesn't it?) that you can't have a proper contest if the other side doesn't even know one is going on.

The court cannot act in your case unless you can properly notify your spouse of the lawsuit. Chapter 6 shows how this is done, but in general terms, either your spouse must sign a Waiver stating that court papers have been received, or else the papers must be served properly by a Sheriff. If your spouse is on active military duty, then the only way you can do your own divorce is if your spouse will sign the Waiver. If your spouse successfully avoids service, or if your spouse is on active military duty and refuses to sign a Waiver, you will need the help of an attorney to proceed with your case.

If your spouse is long gone and all attempts to locate him/her have failed, you are in for a little more work and expense. The law still requires that the missing spouse be given proper notice, but says you can do that by publishing your Citation in a newspaper. You can find forms and instructions for "Citation by Publication" or "Citation by Posting" on the CD that comes with this book. You can also download them for $10.00 at **www. nolodivorce.com/TX,** or call Nolo at **(800) 464-5502,** or order by mail using the order form in the back of this book.

Proper notice means, among other things, that your spouse gets a copy of your Petition, and so can be presumed to know what the suit is about and more or less what you want. After proper notice, a lawsuit can go one of three ways:
- by agreement—parties agree in writing on property, debts, support, parenting.
- by default—the Respondent does nothing; Petitioner completes the case alone.
- by contest—the parties take the case to court and fight for a judicial decision.

The best and easiest way is if you work it out by written agreement, of course. The hardest way is where your spouse gets an attorney and files an Answer on time and you end up in a legal battle. The most common way is by default.

e) Waiting periods

Waiting period before the hearing. The hearing is the time when you get your divorce, but you cannot rush right into it. After filing your Petition, you must wait at least 60 days before you have your hearing. Because of the way the law is worded, the 60-day period can sometimes be tricky to compute, so many lawyers consider it good practice to play it safe by waiting two months and two weeks. If your spouse signs a Waiver, this is the only waiting period that must be satisfied before the hearing.

If your spouse was "served," there are three different waiting periods, all of which must be satisfied. You must not have your hearing sooner than:

1) two months plus two weeks from the date you filed your Petition, *and*
2) 27 days from the date your spouse was served, *and*
3) 12 days from the date the Officer's Return (on the Citation) is filed with the District Clerk (chapter 6).

Please note that these times include a safety margin to cover possible problems with computing time "legally."

Waiting to remarry. You are not free to marry anyone else (except the person you just divorced) for 30 days after the judge orders your divorce.

f) Change of name

In a divorce case, if it is requested by either party, the judge will change the name of either spouse. In actual practice, this rule is almost always used to restore a former name to the wife, but the way the law reads, you can change the name of either spouse to any name they used before. The court *must* grant your name change request unless they state in the Decree a reason for denying the change. They may no longer deny a change of name just to keep the last names of the parents and children the same.

4. How to start a divorce—Petitioners and Respondents

The Petitioner and the Respondent. Every divorce starts with a Petition. The Petitioner is the person who first files papers and gets the case started. The Respondent is the other party. A Response need not be filed, but it is a good idea, otherwise the inactive person has little say about when or how the divorce is completed, unless there is already a written agreement. In general, the more both parties participate, the better. After a Response is filed, the divorce can be completed only by written agreement or court trial. Agreement is better.

Equality. Once a Response is filed, Respondent has equal standing and there is no legal difference between the parties or their rights, and either party can take any available legal step. Where instructions in this book indicate "Petitioner," Respondent can substitute "Respondent" and take the same action.

The Petition. To get your case started, you file a Petition and serve it on your spouse or partner. The only thing you need to know before you do this is that you want to start a divorce. The issues can all be sorted out and resolved later. On the other hand, it wouldn't hurt to read through Part One before you start.

Advantages to serving the Petition:
- Starts the clock ticking on waiting periods.
- Causes automatic restraining orders to take effect.
- Helps establish the date of separation.
- Has psychological value for Petitioner and tells Respondent a divorce is really going to happen.

Possible downside. Serving papers can upset the Respondent and stir up conflict if you don't properly prepare the Respondent ahead of time.

Getting a smooth start. Unless your Ex is an abuser/controller, you will probably want to start things off as nicely as possible. An abrupt start will probably increase conflict, as an upset spouse is more likely to run to an attorney who will probably make your case more complicated. So take some time to prepare your Ex and let him/her get used to the idea that a divorce is about to start. If you aren't comfortable discussing things in person, write a nice letter. Let your spouse know you are committed to working out a settlement that you can both agree to and live with. Unless you are under time pressure, don't serve your Summons and Petition until your partner seems ready to receive the papers calmly.

5. Three ways to get it done (see map on next page)

After you file your Petition, there are only three ways you can get your Divorce Decree: (1) by default, (2) by contest, or (3) by written agreement.

MAP – How to get there from here

(Discussion in section 5)

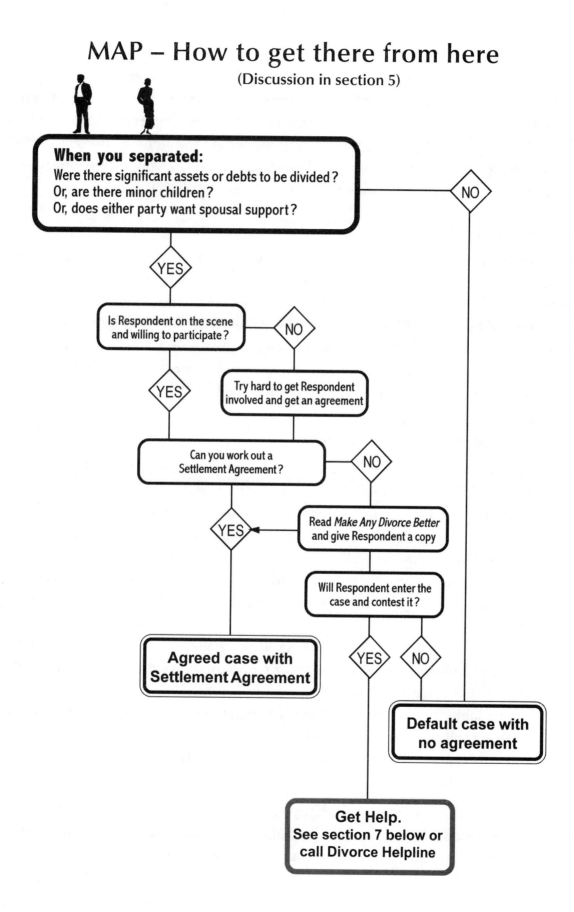

When you separated:
Were there significant assets or debts to be divided?
Or, are there minor children?
Or, does either party want spousal support?

NO

YES

Is Respondent on the scene and willing to participate?

NO

Try hard to get Respondent involved and get an agreement

YES

Can you work out a Settlement Agreement?

NO

Read *Make Any Divorce Better* and give Respondent a copy

YES

Will Respondent enter the case and contest it?

YES   NO

Agreed case with Settlement Agreement

Default case with no agreement

Get Help.
See section 7 below or call Divorce Helpline

The default divorce

In a default case, Respondent is served with the Petition but does nothing. No Response is filed, so the case is completed by default, without participation by Respondent. Default should be used only if you have little property or debts, no children, and no need for spousal or partner support, or where Respondent is long gone or doesn't care to participate. If Respondent is around and cares, you'll need to work out an agreement, otherwise you'll have a complicated contested case to resolve all issues in court.

The contested divorce

If a Response is filed, you can complete your divorce only by written agreement or by taking the case to court and having a judge decide issues that you can't settle. Until there is an agreement, your case is *technically* considered to be contested. Whether or not there is a battle and a lot of legal activity depends on how you go about solving problems and reaching agreement. If you have problems reaching agreement, read *Make Any Divorce Better.* If you find yourself headed into a court battle, get help. Call Divorce Helpline at (800) 359-7004 or see section 8 below.

Divorce by settlement agreement

When the problems are all solved and you finally reach an agreement, one of the parties files a Waiver (chapter 6A) and steps out. The case is now uncontested and sails through. If your spouse is in the picture and you have children, significant property or debts, or you need to arrange spousal support, then you should make *every* effort to reach a written agreement on all issues. Look what you gain:

- You can be certain exactly what the orders in the Decree of Divorce will be;
- You can complete your case by mail and almost certainly won't have to go to court;
- Both parties participate, so the Respondent can feel confident about letting the divorce go through without contest or representation because the terms of the Decree of Divorce are all settled;
- It invariably leads to better relations with your ex-spouse or partner. Where there are children, this is extremely important; and
- You are far more likely to get compliance with terms of the divorce after the Decree of Divorce.

These advantages are so important that you should struggle long and hard to work out an agreement, with or without the help of a mediator or collaborative law attorney (section 8). Chapter E discusses written agreements in detail.

6. Solving divorce problems

The steps you take to make your case go more smoothly depend on what your situation is right at this moment. Five divorce profiles are described below with steps you should take in each situation. See which profile best fits you.

Early cases

You haven't broken up yet, or broke up only recently. This is good, because the earlier you start, the easier it is to heal wounds and lay a foundation for a smoother trip. The way you go about doing things now will have a powerful influence on how things work out in your future—for better or worse.

Your goal is to solve problems and settle issues without taking problems to court or spending much (if any) time in a lawyer's office. Your goal is to end up with an Easy Case (below).

Here are steps you can take to achieve these goals.

- Go to **www.nolodivorce.com** and get my *Free Guide to a Better Divorce*. It offers a mine of information with links to free articles like those mentioned below. The articles can be found in the Reading Room at my web site.
- Read my article, "The Good Divorce," so you will have a model to keep in mind and an idea of things you can try to accomplish to keep your divorce peaceful.
- Read my "Pre-divorce Checklist" and start working on those items.
- Read Part One of this book to learn about divorce laws, and skim Part Two to get a sense of how divorce paperwork is done.
- Get my book, *Make Any Divorce Better*, and learn specific things you can do to smooth things out. Get a copy for your Ex, too, so you can discuss ideas in it.
- **Do not talk to your spouse about divorce** until you learn how to reduce conflict, create a foundation for negotiation, and negotiate effectively.
- **Do not go to an attorney** until you are better informed and prepared—unless, that is, you face an emergency as described in section 7 below.

Before you visit an attorney, you should gather and organize all the facts and documents in your case as described in the Early and Easy case profiles below. Also read section 8 below to learn what you can and cannot expect from various types of attorneys and other professional services.

Easy cases

If your spouse won't come to court to oppose you, you've got an easy case. It could be because he/she is gone, doesn't care, or because you are able to sit down and agree on terms. All that's left is to file papers and go through some red tape to get a Decree of Divorce. You can do the paperwork yourself with this book or get it done inexpensively by negotiating a low price with an attorney. Call Divorce Helpline.

Spouse on board? It's very difficult to divide major assets or arrange parenting without your spouse's participation, so your goal is to settle things in a written settlement agreement. Here are steps you can take to complete an easy case and make sure it stays easy.

- Go to **www.nolodivorce.com** and get my *Free Guide to a Better Divorce*. It offers a mine of information and links to free articles on my site.

- Go to the Reading Room on my site and read my "Pre-divorce Checklist" and start working on those items.

- Read Part One of this book carefully to learn about divorce laws and skim Part Two to get a sense of how divorce paperwork is done. If you have major assets (real estate, retirement funds), it would make sense to have expert advice and an agreement drafted by an attorney, so I recommend that you call Divorce Helpline (800) 359-7004 and find out how they can help you. For other options, read section 8 below. If you're thinking of using online divorce forms, go to the Reading Room at **www.nolodivorce. com** and read my article that explains why online forms are *not* a good idea.

- **Keeping easy cases easy.** Most divorces are delicate and easily stirred up. To learn how to keep an easy case from blowing up into a difficult one, I recommend that each spouse have a copy of *Make Any Divorce Better* and follow specific steps to calm conflict and negotiate effectively. Discuss ideas in it.

- **Get organized.** As soon as you can, organize your facts, gather documents, and start thinking about how to divide community property, how much spousal support will be paid (if any), and how children will be supported and parented. You'll find a set of Divorce Worksheets on the CD that comes with this book. These will help you organize, think about, and discuss the facts and finances in your case. They will definitely save you time and money.

- **A written settlement agreement** is very important in most cases. The simple sample agreement that comes with this book is not ideal for dealing with major assets, but **DealMaker** software is (see inside front cover). **DealMaker** clarifies the many possible options for real estate or retirement funds and also guides you in the creation of a parenting plan if you have minor children. **DealMaker** guides you to enter information and make some decisions, then it writes a sophisticated, professional settlement agreement that you can sign as is or edit with any word processor.

Difficult cases—when things don't go smoothly (or might not)

This profile fits most divorces. Your spouse is in the picture and cares about how things will end up, but you're having some trouble (or you expect to) with discussing and settling terms.

The reason divorce agreements are difficult is almost always personal—bad communication, bad history, bad habits, etc.—and almost never about the law. Neither the law nor lawyers have any tools to help you settle problems that originate in your personal relationship. In fact, the things you can do yourself are far superior to anything a lawyer can do for you.

Your goal is to take specific steps that will make your case smoother and easier, to turn it into an Easy Divorce (above), so you can make a written agreement and do the paperwork yourself or get it done inexpensively. There are a lot of things you can do for yourself to make things better, steps that have helped tens of thousands of couples, so they can help you, too.

Here are the steps you should take.

• Go to **www.nolodivorce.com** and get my *Free Guide to a Better Divorce*. It contains a mine of information with links to my free articles mentioned below, found in the Reading Room at my web site.

• Read my article "The Good Divorce," so you will have a model to keep in mind and an idea of things you can try to accomplish to keep your divorce peaceful.

• Start working on early steps, listed in my "Pre-divorce Checklist."

• Get *Make Any Divorce Better* and learn about the specific things you can do to smooth things out. Get a copy for your Ex, too, so you can discuss ideas in it. Section 7 below discusses strategies for difficult cases.

• **Do not talk to your spouse** about divorce until you learn how to reduce conflict, create a foundation for negotiation, and negotiate effectively.

• **Do not talk to an attorney** until you are informed and prepared—unless, that is, you face an emergency like those described in section 7 below.

• **Organize your facts.** Start now to organize your documents and facts. I created a set of Divorce Worksheets to help you organize, think about, and discuss the facts and finances in your case. They will definitely save you time and money. These worksheets can be found on the CD that comes with this book or can be purchased separately.

- **DealMaker.** Your highest goal is to get a written settlement agreement of all issues in your case. The sample agreement in this book is not ideal for dealing with major or complex assets, but **DealMaker** software is. You'll find a trial version on the CD in the back of this book. **DealMaker** is especially useful for dealing with the many possible options for real estate and retirement funds, and it helps you create a custom parenting plan. DealMaker guides you to enter information and make some decisions, then it writes a sophisticated, professional settlement agreement that you can sign as is or edit with any word processor.

- **Mediation.** If you have trouble working out terms, you don't need an attorney, you need a mediator. Call Divorce Helpline at (800) 359-7004.

- **Collaborative law.** If you want to be represented by an attorney, try to get a collaborative lawyer on both sides. Read more about this in section 8 below. Divorce Helpline does collaborative law as well as arbitration.

- **Arbitration.** If you can't resolve issues in mediation, consider taking your case to arbitration rather than court. It is similar, in that the arbitrator imposes a decision, but the setting is less formal and an arbitrator is paid by the hour, so will take all the time you need to understand the facts about your family and situation. A judge has to move cases along quickly, so will tend to hurry through divorce motions or trials.

Domestic abuse and violence (DV)

DV includes physical attacks, threats, intimidation, verbal attacks (put-downs, insults, undermining your self-confidence) and other efforts to control you. It can be difficult to distinguish between high levels of divorce conflict and forms of domestic abuse and violence. The DV profile is about cases where your spouse is an habitual controller/abuser, someone who has abused repeatedly. These people are not responsive to reason because their need to control or abuse is too strong, so when dealing with an habitual controller/abuser, your only choice is to go somewhere safe and get specialized help.

Safety first. If you fear for the safety of yourself or a child, go somewhere safe where you can't be found. Ask the local police for domestic abuse support groups near you. What you need most now is personal advice and counseling from someone who specializes in domestic abuse.

Legal battle

If you follow my advice, you probably won't end up in a legal battle, but sometimes you simply can't avoid one or you might be in one already. If you're already in a legal battle, or if you can't avoid a battle even after following the steps in *Make Any Divorce Better*, then you have to do what you have to do—get an attorney and fight. If you must fight, you might as well learn how to do it effectively, so welcome to the Battle Group. Keep in mind that this is a legal battle, which is all about business. You do not want to battle on a personal or emotional level. In fact, you will be more effective and healthier if you don't. But you do need to learn:

- How to deal with extreme conflict
- Damage control
- How to protect children
- Winning strategies—hardball or softball?
- How to fight effectively at less expense
- How to choose and use your attorney
- How to fire your attorney (if you want to)

Make Any Divorce Better discusses this information in detail. Also get *How to Solve Divorce Problems*, which discusses all stages of legal battle, so you can either handle them yourself or monitor and supervise your attorney's conduct of your case. This allows you to call the shots and maintain a degree of control over your own case.

If you're in a legal battle, you should make persistent efforts to move your case toward negotiated or mediated agreement, using all the steps discussed in *Make Any Divorce Better*. Discourage legal action or activity that you think is not necessary and instruct your attorney that you want to mediate as soon as possible and be kept informed of every effort to make that happen. Also talk about this directly with your spouse, if possible, either in person or by mail.

7. When you should get some help

Emergencies—when retaining an attorney makes sense

If your situation is described below, read the recommended articles to decide if you need to retain an attorney. If your situation is not described below, you should read Part One of this book and also look through *Make Any Divorce Better*, then take some time to think things over and take the steps I recommend for your type of case.

a) Personal emergencies

- **Fear for the safety of yourself or your child.** If your spouse is an habitual controller/abuser and you fear it will happen again, you need advice from a domestic violence counselor. Ask your local police or Superior Court Clerk's office for a list of local DV support groups and call them to ask for names of people who can advise you and, if necessary, help you find a safe place to stay.

- **Fear of sneak attack.** If you think your spouse might do a sneak attack by filing for court orders for custody and support without discussion or warning, or maybe just take the kids and the money and run, or both, read about strategies in Chapter 5D of *Make Any Divorce Better* and decide if you are going to be defensive or take the offense first.

- **Desperately broke.** If your financial situation is truly desperate—or if your spouse feels this way—go to the Reading Room at **www.nolodivorce.com** and read my article "Funding Your Separation."

- **Parenting children.** Many people run to an attorney because they are afraid they won't get to see their children often enough. If this describes you, go to the Reading Room at **www.nolodivorce.com** and read "Parenting in the Early Stages."

b) Legal emergencies

- **Divorce papers served on you.** This may not be an emergency. If you've only been served with the Summons and Petition that start a divorce action in court and you want to have some say in the outcome, you need to file a Response—see section 8 to read about who can help you do this—before the deadline stated on your papers. If the deadline has passed, call the Superior Court Clerk and ask if you are still able to file a Response even though the deadline has passed. If so, quickly file a Response. If not, you'll need an attorney to help you make a motion to allow you to enter the case late. In either situation, read section 8 below about how to find the right kind of help.

However, if a motion has been filed and a hearing scheduled in the near future to determine support or child custody issues, you need to get an attorney right away to either represent you at the hearing or seek a continuance so you can prepare. Read section 8 about what kind of attorney you want. If you don't have time to get an attorney, show up in court at the time and place indicated on your papers and ask the judge for a continuance so you can get an attorney. Even if you are in litigation, you should read *Make Any Divorce Better* and look for ways to move the action out of court and into mediation.

- **You are already in litigation.** If you are already in a legal struggle with attorneys on both sides, read *Make Any Divorce Better* to learn how the law works and how to guide your case toward negotiation, mediation, or collaborative divorce. If all else fails, arbitration is better than going to court. Get *How to Solve Divorce Problems* so you can see how a contested divorce works and use it to monitor your own attorney's performance. What you do not want is to end up stuck in a court battle where everyone loses but the attorneys.

c) Legal advice—when to get it and from whom

In some situations, you can get a lot of good from a little advice. In *any* case, you can get peace of mind from knowing you are doing things right. A few hundred dollars for advice may not seem unreasonable when weighed against the value of your property, debts, possible tax savings, all future support payments, and the importance of a good parenting plan. You can often save more than you spend.

If you have any of the situations listed below in your case, you have good reason to get some legal advice. Section 8 suggests who to go to.

Property
- The division of assets and debts is not equal.
- A major asset is being divided or sold—avoiding capital gains problems.
- You aren't sure how to value some assets, such as a business or a professional practice, etc.
- You have stock options—valuation, division, relationship to child and spousal (partner) support.
- Separate and community money was mixed together in a major asset.
- Pension or retirement funds accumulated at least in part during marriage—how to value and how to divide without penalty.

Debts
- You have lots of debts and/or you want to protect yourself from your spouse's debts.
- Either party might declare bankruptcy.
- Joint credit card or other accounts have not been not closed.

Your spouse (solutions are discussed at length in *Make Any Divorce Better*)
- You can't agree about important issues.
- You can't get information from your spouse about income, assets, debts.
- You suspect your spouse might be hiding assets.

Children

- There is disagreement over parenting arrangements.
- One parent doesn't want the other to move.
- One parent earns much more than the other—consider saving on taxes by arranging for family support instead of child support.
- There are special needs or health problems.

Spousal or partner support

- You have been married five years or more.
- There is more than 20% difference in incomes.
- One spouse is not self-supporting.
- One spouse put the other through school or training.
- You have preschool children.
- There are special needs or health problems.

Personal

- With a good income and busy schedule, you would be better off if someone else did the paperwork.
- You want to be sure you're doing the right thing and know things are being done correctly.
- You don't understand your situation or what to do about it.
- You want help and suggestions for how to negotiate with your spouse.

8.   Who can help?

Friends and relatives are the least reliable sources of advice. Accept all the moral support you can get, but when they give you advice, just smile and say, "Thank you," but do not take it to heart. Also be wary of "common knowledge." If you didn't get it from this book or a family law attorney in Texas, *don't trust it!* Just because you like or trust someone doesn't make them right.

Online divorce services

There are services on the Internet where you can fill out divorce forms for anywhere from zero to $250 or more. What's wrong with that? Well, if it was a good idea, we would have done it long ago, but it is not a good idea. What you really want is someone you can meet with face to face and discuss the options for your case. Here's what online services don't tell you:

Not enough information. Divorce is not about filling out forms—it is about understanding your situation and making decisions. To fill out forms, you need to know what it means to check one box rather than another or file one form rather than another. You need to know where you are in the paperwork, what's going on, where you are going. At all online services we have reviewed, this information is either totally inadequate or completely missing. Not good.

Limited and incomplete. These services have one fixed way to do cases that does not cover a wide variety of situations. You can easily discover partway through that your case does not fit their pattern. Some services get you started but do not complete the case or do not provide important options.

Inflexible. Once you start to fill out the forms, you are stuck on a very long path that you can't get off. It is not easy, maybe not possible, to jump about from one form or page to another. What's worse, you can't step back and get a long view, so you are forced to work without a good understanding of what's going on, where you are in the process, where you are trying to go, or why you are doing things their way.

The better option. If you and your Ex can agree on how to divide property, whether or not there will be alimony and, if you have minor children, how they will be supported and parented after your separation, then you can use this book to complete your forms, or find someone in a city near you who will complete your paperwork for relatively little, a few hundred dollars. Get a copy of our **DealMaker** software (inside front cover) and make a settlement agreement. Then go on the Internet and search for "Divorce Assistance" plus the name of a city near you, or call lots of attorneys and explain that you have a settlement agreement and only need paperwork completed and ask how much this will cost. Keep calling until you get a price that seems reasonable.

Mediators

If you can't work out an agreement on your own, you should try mediation. A mediator can help you communicate, balance the negotiating power, develop options you haven't thought of, solve problems, break through any impasse and help you reach a fair agreement. If your problems are primarily personal or about parenting, a non-attorney mediator can be used, but if property or legal issues are involved, it might be best to select a family law attorney-mediator.

Mediation is not just for friendly divorces. Angry, conflicted couples are especially in need of mediation and stand to gain the most, particularly if they have children. Mediation can be very effective, even in cases with high conflict, when conducted by a good family law attorney-mediator like those at Divorce Helpline. If the parties can't even agree to try mediation, we are willing to contact the other side and try to arrange a meeting. Divorce Helpline works by phone, email, video-conference, and fax throughout Texas. We can even do telephone mediation, which can be surprisingly effective and a lifesaver if parties can't meet at one location in person.

Lawyers

Advice. Unless you expect (or want) a legal battle, the best place to get advice is from a family law attorney who mostly does mediation rather than litigation. This way, you are more likely to get practical advice designed to solve problems rather than contentious advice that can lead you to court.

Traditional lawyers who *specialize* in divorce and work in the court system know a lot that could help you, but, because of the way the system works and the way lawyers work, they will almost certainly create unnecessary conflict and expense if you retain one. Unfortunately, getting information and advice from traditional attorneys without retaining them can be tricky, because they don't really want to help you help yourself; they want to be retained to do it all.

Attorneys will frequently do the first interview for a fairly small fee, but too often they spend that time convincing you that you need them to handle your case. Hourly rates can run from $150 to $450, but $175–$350 per hour is normal. Most attorneys require a retainer—$1,200 to $5,000 is typical—but the amount doesn't matter because the final bill will be *much* higher. Few attorneys will give you a definite maximum figure for the whole job. You are doing *very* well if you end up spending less than $5,000 *per spouse* on the *simplest* case. The average in urban areas when both spouses are represented is *well* over $18,000 *per spouse*, but couples with larger estates can expect costs to run into tens or hundreds of thousands of dollars—*per spouse!*

Limited representation. A small but growing number of lawyers are offering representation limited to specific tasks or portions of your case while you keep overall responsibility. For example, they will represent you only to draft your agreement, or only to appear in court if you are asked to show up there for some reason, or only to file and appear on one motion. If you need a bit of service from a family law attorney, call around and ask if they offer "limited representation" or "unbundling," the two names by which this service is known. Better yet, call Divorce Helpline, as we've been doing this sort of thing since 1990.

Attorney-mediators. See "Mediators" above. When you're looking for advice, it would be best to get it from an attorney who does mostly mediation, as the advice you get is more likely to be practical and about solving problems rather than going to court.

Collaborative divorce. Increasingly popular, spouses and their attorneys pledge in writing not go to court or threaten to go to court as a way to solve problems. Instead, they will use advice, negotiation, and mediation to reach a settlement. If there's no settlement, the spouses will have to get different attorneys to take the case into litigation. In some cases, the collaborative team might include other professionals, such as a divorce coach, family counselor, child specialist, accountant, or financial planner. Collaborative divorce has a good track record and, even with all the professional services you get, it will still cost less than a court battle.

Divorce Helpline

Divorce Helpline was created to change the way attorneys practice in divorce cases and to provide expert support for people who are doing their own. Divorce Helpline is operated by the law offices of Sherman, Naraghi, Woodcock & Pipersky. Texas cases are handled and supervised by Texas attorney Bruce Naraghi. Divorce Helpline will not litigate (go to court) because we don't believe in it. Instead, our expert family law attorneys work exclusively as your guide and assistant, helping you plan, solve problems, and reach a fair settlement. We offer advice, mediation, arbitration, and collaborative law, working by telephone throughout Texas. Divorce Helpline attorneys are trained in mediation and communication and are good at solving problems. We'll answer your questions, but we can do a better job for you when we do the *whole* case—the paperwork and the settlement agreement—as well as giving you advice. That way we have *all* the information, not just the small bit you are asking about. When we do the whole case, we often find problems to solve and ways to save money that people don't know to ask about. Our methods have proven to be highly successful and very affordable. Learn more about Divorce Helpline, including our rates and services, at www.divorcehelp.com, or call (800) 359-7004 for a free explanation of how we work and how we can help you.

9. Some Common Questions and Answers

• **How much will it cost to do your own divorce?** The filing fees are set from time to time by law, and costs vary slightly from one county to another. These days, it costs as much as $200 to file papers in a case where your spouse signs a Waiver of the Citation, and as much as $50 more if the Citation must be issued, plus the Sheriff's fee (about $60) for serving the Citation on your spouse. Add to this a few dollars for photocopies and postage, and that's it. If you were to hire an attorney or a typist or buy a kit, you would still have to pay these fees in addition to the base cost. You'll be hard pressed to find a better bargain than this book.

• **How long will it take?** The shortest possible time to complete a divorce is 61 days from the filing of the Petition, but plan on a bit longer, say three months. It is okay to take longer if you are in no hurry.

• **What if we reconcile?** If you file a divorce Petition and later reconcile and change your mind, just let it lie there. Within a few months, it will be dismissed for lack of prosecution, after a written notice from the clerk.

• **When can I remarry?** After your final Decree of divorce is ordered, you must wait at least 30 days before marrying anyone other than the spouse you just divorced.

• **What about alimony?** In 1995, Texas finally joined the other 49 states in granting alimony (called spousal maintenance) upon divorce. It is a stingy little law, with severe limitations on amount and duration that are described in more detail in chapter D. However, the spouses are free to reach almost any kind of agreement about alimony in a written marital settlement agreement and the courts will almost certainly go along with it.

• **What if the wife is pregnant?** You should wait until the child is born to get your divorce. Judges do not like to see a child born out of wedlock, and enforcing child support could be a problem. If you can't wait, see an attorney.

• **Am I liable for my spouse's bills?** During the marriage (even if you are separated), both spouses are liable for the bills of the other. After the divorce, the parties are responsible only for their own bills.

• **What if I am common-law married?** Three elements must exist to form a common-law marriage: 1) an agreement to be married (whether explicit or implied); 2) after the agreement, you lived together as husband and wife; and 3) you represented to others that you were husband and wife. If your marriage is common-law, the same rules for divorce apply to you as to couples married in a ceremony. However, if you believe you are common-law married, you have only two years from the date you separate to file for divorce. If neither party files within that time, it is presumed that no common-law marriage existed, and you won't be able to use this book to get a divorce.

- **Does divorce have tax consequences?** Yes. Almost every aspect of divorce could possibly have important tax consequences. Depending upon what property and income you have, you could possibly save a lot of money by seeing a tax expert, especially before making a marital settlement agreement. There are also rules you should know about if you have children. The tax rules are numerous and they change frequently, but fortunately there is an excellent little booklet that tells you everything you should know, and it is absolutely free. Simply call your local Internal Revenue Service office and ask for IRS publication 504, "Divorced or Separated Individuals."

10. Looking ahead

As mentioned in section 4 above, you can file your Petition and serve it at any time, assuming you have arranged for a smooth start by preparing your spouse or partner to receive it. You can then take some time to make decisions and work out the details about your property, support, and children. We discuss the basic rules of these subjects in chapters B, C, and D. Chapter E shows you how everything can be wrapped up in a settlement agreement once you get things worked out. If you have a more complex estate, real estate, or retirement funds, you should get **DealMaker** software (inside front cover), which uses the power of software to make it easy for you to deal with the many options available for major assets. You just enter requested information, make requested decisions, and **DealMaker** drafts a comprehensive settlement agreement that you can sign as is or edit in any full-featured word processor.

Preparation. Eventually, to complete your divorce you will have to create a complete list of all of your assets and debts, and it will be extremely useful if you start doing that now. Start filling out the worksheets that come on the CD with this book and gather all documents and records related to your assets, debts, and family. Getting prepared in this manner will help organize your facts, your documents, and your thinking. It will suggest other information or questions you might have.

If you have trouble getting information you need, read "Getting the Information You Need," which is in the appendix in *Make Any Divorce Better.*

Go to my web site, **www.nolodivorce.com**, look in the Reading Room, get the free article, "Pre-divorce Checklist," and start working on those items right away.

Study the Decree of Divorce. While you are reading through the next few chapters, at some point you should jump ahead to chapter 7 and take a look at the Decree. Read the language in the various orders that are used in the Decree so you can understand where all this information you are reading about will end up. Then you'll have a better idea of where you are going while reading about how to get there.

B. Dividing Property and Debts

One of the most important parts of a divorce action is dividing the property and debts (the estate) of the marriage. One of the most important services of an attorney is going over your estate with you to see what you own, what you owe, and how it can all be divided. The attorney will have an eye to getting you, the client, the best deal possible. Unless you have a large or complicated estate, this book will tell you how to understand your own estate and decide for yourself how to divide it.

1. Cases where there is no property

Do not conclude that you have no property without going over the checklist in section 3 to make sure that you have thought of everything.

Cases without property are very easy to do, because you merely tell the court that there is no significant property to be divided, and the court does nothing. There will be but little inquiry into your property and no orders about it.

Several types of cases can be handled this way. Perhaps there's not enough property to worry about, or maybe your spouse is long gone or doesn't care, so has abandoned what little property there is to you. Or maybe you have already divided things between you, so at the time you file there is nothing left to be divided by the court. In cases like these, you may decide that you do not need or want the court to make orders about the division of your property.

Do not use this approach if there is any chance of future argument about property of any significant value, or where there is real estate that has not yet been divided correctly, or where there is a community interest in a pension plan.

2. Cases where there is some property

Make sure you understand your marital estate and know all that it contains. Read section 3 and go over the checklist very carefully to make sure you have thought of everything. Be sure to include property acquired anywhere else that would have been community property had it been acquired in Texas. If you think it likely that your spouse has hidden assets that you don't know and can't find out about, then you might benefit from the services of an attorney who can get the spouse in court and under order to reveal everything.

If at the time of your divorce your estate contains property or bills of any significant value, then you will want to have things divided properly as part of the divorce.

Property can be divided by the parties or by a judge. Spouses can agree to divide their property any way they see fit. If this is completed before the Petition is filed, then there is no community property to divide and the case will be very easy to process. If there is some community property but no agreement at the time of filing, then that property must be listed in the Petition. If by the time of the court hearing there is still no agreement, the property will be divided by the judge. In this case, neither spouse will be entirely in control of how the property gets divided, although the judge will be strongly influenced by the suggestions of the Petition or the spouse in court.

When thinking about dividing your property, keep in mind that getting the last cent may not be your best or highest goal. Consider the children, if any, the relative earning ability of each of you, your general situation, fairness, and other such things. Try to consider what will be best for everyone, both now and in the future.

If you have a lot of property, you might want to think about getting professional advice from an accountant or lawyer. A professional, such as those at Divorce Helpline, can tell you how to locate it, value it, divide it, transfer it, and generally protect your interests.

3. Understanding your estate

a) The marital estate: separate and community property defined

A marriage has three estates: the separate property of husband, the separate property of wife, and community property belonging to both. While a divorce decree should clarify the separate property of each spouse, only community property (CP) needs to be divided in a divorce, since separate property (SP) already belongs to each spouse individually. The first step, then, is to determine what property in the marital estate is CP, SP, or a combination of the two. In section 4, we discuss how CP is divided.

Checklist. Use the checklist shown here to organize your thinking about the property and bills in your marital estate. Make a few blank copies before you start filling it out. Better yet, our companion CD has the same checklist in the Forms Etc folder, a PDF version with fields that you can fill out on any computer.

Community property is any property other than SP, no matter where it is located, that was acquired by either spouse during the marriage. Property owned by either spouse during the marriage or at the time of the dissolution is **presumed** to be community property. Even if the spouses have been separated for years, the earnings and debts of each spouse are community property until the divorce is ordered.

Property checklist and worksheet

Item	Market value	Amount owed	Net value	Proposed division

1. Real Estate
    family home
    rental property
    recreation property
    other				

2. Household goods, furniture, and appliances				
3. Jewelry, antiques, art, collections, coins, etc.				
4. Vehicles, boats, trailers (get license and ID numbers)				
5. Cash on hand, and savings, checking, credit union accounts (get account numbers)				

Property checklist and worksheet (continued)

Item	Market value	Amount owed	Net value	Proposed division
6. Life insurance with cash value (get policy numbers)				
7. Equipment, machinery, and livestock				
8. Stocks, bonds, secured notes				
9. Retirement/pension plans, profit-sharing plans, annuities				
10. Tax refunds due, accounts receivable, unsecured notes				
11. Partnerships, business interests				
12. Other assets				

13. List all other debts, taxes due, bills:

To whom due   **What for**   **Balance**

Separate property is property owned before marriage, acquired during marriage by gift or inheritance directed to just one spouse, and recovery for injury suffered during marriage, except recovery for loss of earning capacity during the marriage. Without some clear agreement otherwise, SP that is mixed and mingled with CP tends to lose its separate quality. For the sake of clarity, SP of significant value or personal meaning should be listed in your Petition and in any agreement between the spouses.

In case there's a disagreement as to what is SP, the degree of proof required to establish that the property is separate is "clear and convincing evidence." This means you must be able to trace and clearly identify the property claimed as separate, say by showing that it was purchased with SP funds. If the identity of SP is ambiguous or intermingled with CP, you will probably need the assistance of a family law attorney. You can call Divorce Helpline for advice or assistance.

b) When funds flow between marital estates

During marriage, it is not uncommon for funds to flow between marital estates, that is, from separate to community or vice-versa. Unless there is a pre- or post-marital contract that states otherwise, then to the extent it can be made clear with records, one marital estate might have a claim against another for reimbursement that matures on dissolution. Prior to September 1, 2009, Texas had a complicated law called "Economic Contribution," which has been repealed and now applies only to cases filed before the new law took effect. If your case was filed before that date and you think you might have a claim not covered below, get help. Call Divorce Helpline.

Reimbursement. Under the new law, a claim for reimbursement includes:

1. Payment by one marital estate of unsecured liabilities of another marital estate;
2. Inadequate compensation for the time, toil, talent, and effort of a spouse by a business entity under the control and direction of that spouse;
3. The reduction of the principal amount of a debt secured by a lien on property owned before marriage, to the extent the debt existed at the time of marriage;
4. The reduction of the principal amount of a debt secured by a lien on property received by a spouse by gift, devise, or descent during a marriage, to the extent the debt existed at the time the property was received;
5. The reduction of the principal amount of that part of a debt, including a home equity loan that was:
    a. incurred during a marriage;
    b. secured by a lien on property; and
    c. incurred for the acquisition of, or for capital improvements to, property;

6. The reduction of the principal amount of that part of a debt that was:
   a. incurred during a marriage;
   b. secured by a lien on property owned by a spouse;
   c. for which the creditor agreed to look for repayment solely to the separate marital estate of the spouse on whose property the lien attached; and
   d. incurred for the acquisition of, or for capital improvements to, property;
7. The refinancing of the principal amount described by Subdivisions (3)-(6), to the extent the refinancing reduces that principal amount in a manner described by the applicable subdivision;
8. Capital improvements to property other than by incurring debt; and
9. The reduction by the community property estate of an unsecured debt incurred by the separate estate of one of the spouses.

Claims for reimbursement can be offset against each other if the parties agree or a court decides it is appropriate. Any benefit for the use and enjoyment of property may be offset against a claim for reimbursement for expenditures to benefit a marital estate, except a separate estate of a spouse may *not* claim an offset for use and enjoyment of a primary or secondary residence owned wholly or partly by the separate estate against contributions made by the community estate to the separate estate. If reimbursement is sought for funds used to improve another marital estate, the court is to use the standard of enhancement of value.

Claims are determined on equitable principles and it is entirely in the discretion of the judge whether to recognize a claim, taking into account all circumstances and having due regard for the rights of each spouse and any children of their marriage—another reason why it's better and safer to settle it between you.

Nonreimbursable claims. The court will not recognize a marital estate's claim for reimbursement for:
1. The payment of child support, alimony, or spousal maintenance;
2. The living expenses of a spouse or child of a spouse;
3. Contributions of property of little value;
4. The payment of a liability of small amount; or
5. A student loan owed by a spouse.

If you suspect you have a potential claim for reimbursement but find this difficult, you might want to get legal advice from a family law specialist. Call Divorce Helpline.

c) Bills and liabilities of the spouses

If you or your spouse, or both of you, accumulated debts during your marriage, these are community debts that will have to be valued and divided along with the property.

Important. Orders of the court and agreements between spouses about who is to pay bills do not in any way affect people you owe. If you owed money to someone before the divorce and your spouse is ordered to pay the bill but does not, then you still owe the money. The creditor can come after you or repossess the property. Your spouse may be in contempt of court, for all the good that does you.

Between marriage and divorce, spouses are liable for each other's debts. This means that if your spouse moved away five years ago, hasn't been heard from since, and bought some shoes last month, the shoe store can come to you for payment if the bill is not paid by your spouse. This unnecessary and unfortunate rule is the reason many people are in a big hurry to get their divorce over with.

As soon as you separate, close all joint accounts and notify all creditors in writing that you will no longer be responsible for the debts of your spouse.

d) Pension and retirement plans

There are often benefits to employment beyond wages, including accrued rights in a profit-sharing plan, company or government pension plans, Keoghs, 401(k) and 403(b) plans, Individual Retirement Accounts (IRAs), SEP IRAs, Tax Sheltered Annuities (TSAs), and Employee Stock Option plans (ESOPs). If either spouse was a participant in such a plan during the marriage, then some part of that plan is community property that *must* be dealt with as part of the divorce.

This area can be difficult, so if you read through the material below and get confused, don't feel bad—it confuses most lawyers too! After you read this section, if you have questions or want advice, call Divorce Helpline.

Social Security is not community property and not subject to division by a court. It is a federal program with its own rules, so contact the Social Security Administration about your rights after divorce. Note that benefits accrue to spouses of a marriage that lasted at least 10 years, so if you are approaching that deadline, don't rush into a Judgment that could conveniently be postponed.

Military and Federal Pensions. Military retirement pay and federal civil service benefits can be community property and subject to division in state courts. Spouses of marriages that last through 10 years or more of military service gain advantages in the enforcement of pension awards. Former spouses of marriages that lasted through at least 20 years of active military service are entitled to commissary and PX benefits. Don't be hasty with your divorce if you are approaching a 10- or 20-year deadline. A retiring military spouse can be bound by a written agreement to designate a former spouse as beneficiary under a Survivor Benefit Plan (SBP) if the agreement is incorporated, ratified, or approved in a court order incident to divorce, and if the Secretary concerned receives a request from the former spouse, along with the agreement and court order.

Must be valued correctly. If the community has an interest in a retirement fund or plan, you need to know how much that interest is worth.

- If your plan is a tax-deferred savings account like a 401(k), the total value is probably the figure shown on the summary statement. *The community share* in such a fund is equal to the number of married years the employee-spouse was part of the plan, divided by the total number of years of employment when the marriage is dissolved. Multiply the current worth of the pension plan at time of divorce by this ratio to determine the current value of the community interest—that is the amount subject to division at the time of divorce.

- For defined benefit plans where you have to wait for a certain age or number of years of employment to begin receiving payments, it requires an expert to say how much the plan and the community interest are worth. You must have your plan appraised by a professional pension actuary—it will be money well spent! If you call around to find one, be sure to ask if they do "present buy-out appraisals of community interest in a pension plan." You might also ask how many they do each year. Most lawyers would not be capable of doing it correctly, nor would most accountants. If you need an appraisal of a pension plan, call Divorce Helpline for a referral.

Joinder. If the community has an interest in one or more pension plans or retirement funds, then unless you are already completely certain that the entire plan or fund will be awarded to the employee-spouse, you need to join each plan or fund to your case to freeze the funds and make sure they are not improperly withdrawn or transferred before the matter is settled correctly in a judgment. So, with the exception of federal government plans and individual IRA accounts (not including SEP IRAs), when you file your Petition, or as soon after as possible, you should also join each plan or fund. You will need help doing this, so call Divorce Helpline for assistance.

How to deal with a pension plan when doing your own divorce. Because of the complexities involved with retirement and pension funds, if you are going to have a settlement agreement, we recommend that you use DealMaker instead of the simple sample agreement in chapter 6.

The following methods can be used either to settle the pension matter now or to put it off for later.

1) The waiver can be used if the community interest is truly worth very little. The non-employee-spouse simply gives up, in a settlement agreement, all interest in the employee's pension fund.

2) The trade-off (present day buy-out) is a clean and easy way to divide a pension fund; courts like it, and it has no immediate tax consequences. By this method, one spouse trades his/her interest in the employee-spouse's pension plan for something else of equal value, such as a larger share of the family home or a promissory note. Be careful—insist that any note be secured, preferably with a Trust Deed on real property.

Note that the employee-spouse trades hard dollars in the present for something that *might* be collected if he or she stays employed long enough and lives long enough to collect. The employee-spouse will pay taxes on that future income while the other spouse pays no taxes on the trade. However, the employee-spouse may need the entire pension to live on after retirement, so it may be better to pay now rather than have less to live on later. Or maybe the community interest is relatively low and easy to pay for now, just to get things wrapped up cleanly.

3) The payoff (division into two accounts) awards present ownership of a share of *future* pension rights (when they come due) to the non-employee-spouse. Transfers following a payoff *must* be done in strict accordance with IRS rules, or you might suffer an *immediate* tax liability. This method costs several hundred dollars for a special order called a QDRO (see below). The non-employee-spouse may have to wait for his/her share, and the employee-spouse will have a smaller pension check to live on. It is most appropriate in long marriages where the pension is the only or largest asset. Sometimes the employee-spouse will use it to reduce or eliminate spousal support payments.

QDROs. To divide a pension plan or retirement fund, you need a Qualified Domestic Relations Order (QDRO), which is like an official title or "pink slip" to a share of the pension fund, 401(k), or annuity. This *must* be done at the same time or before the Judgment is signed or the non-employee-spouse could lose out. Besides, plan or fund administrators will probably not release funds without a proper order that meets their highly specific requirements.

Two different plans require two joinders (see above) and two QDROs. One pension plan with multiple parts may require more than one QDRO. QDRO orders are difficult to draft and any mistake could be very expensive, so we *strongly* recommend that you call Divorce Helpline or an attorney with a lot of pension fund experience to see if there is some way to get what you want *safely* without having to prepare a QDRO, or to prepare a QDRO for you. Don't take a chance with such an important matter—get expert assistance . It will be worth it.

Death benefits. Divorce automatically removes a spouse as beneficiary under some plans but not others, so the employee-spouse should notify the plan of the divorce and name a new beneficiary. The non-employee-spouse may want to be continued under the plan, but it is usually better to value this part of the plan separately and replace it with an annuity or life insurance of equal value and cover the cost in the settlement agreement, perhaps with a small increase in spousal support.

Be careful with pension plans and retirement funds as there are often tax consequences and penalties if pensions or 401(k)s are not correctly divided or if withdrawals are made before retirement age. Don't touch a fund without making sure your changes won't end up costing you. If you want advice about how to deal with pensions or retirement funds, or help deciding what's best for you, call Divorce Helpline. Our attorneys will help you achieve a fair division of your pension funds in the best and safest way. We can arrange a valuation for you and do the paperwork necessary to make your plans work correctly.

e) The family home and other real estate

If you and your spouse own your home or other real property, then you must decide how to divide it. Some likely alternatives are to sell it and split the proceeds; have one spouse transfer it outright to the other; or have one spouse transfer it to the other in return for something, such as other property, or a note for some amount to be paid in the future (at some specific date or upon some specified event, such as when the kids are grown, if and when the house is sold, the spouse moves out of it, or any other that you can agree to). In a slow market, you can defer the sale and own it together as tenants-in-common until you decide the time is right to sell it.

Before deciding what to do about real property, you need to know how much of it you actually own—your "equity," which is the difference between what you can get for it on the current market less mortgages, liens, and the cost of selling it. You can find out the current market value of your property by consulting a professional real estate appraiser. This will cost some money, so call around for prices. You would also do fairly well by calling in a few local real estate agents, but this may not be as accurate. Once you have figured the market value, deduct the amounts you owe on it and the commission for the real estate agents. If you don't sell it yourself, they will get six to eight percent. Add on a few hundred dollars for miscellaneous expenses.

The divorce will be much easier if you can settle the matter of the real estate and transfer it before you file the Petition. That way you won't have to list the house and make orders about it in your Decree. Agreements about real property are not enforceable unless they are in writing. In order to actually transfer the home from joint ownership by both spouses into sole ownership of one spouse, you need to make a deed from one spouse to the other, then have that deed signed before a Notary and recorded in the county where the property is located. Similarly, if a note is to be assumed, then it too must be properly drawn up, signed, and recorded. There will be a small fee for recording and maybe a transfer tax. If you cannot make up your own deed or note from forms available at a stationer's, then you should seek assistance from a title company, bank, real estate broker, or attorney. Call around. A form for transferring the property between spouses is included with the forms in the back of this book.

If you do not transfer the home before the Petition is filed, then it must be listed with your other property. If it is still not transferred by the time of the hearing, or settled by written agreement, the judge will divide it along with all the other listed property. In the Petition and Decree, the property should be listed by both its common address and legal description (as on the deed). The judge can award the house to one spouse, or order it sold and the proceeds divided in some particular way. It is much better if the spouses take care of it their own way before the Petition is filed.

Because the time and manner of transfer can have tax consequences, it can benefit spouses to cooperate over the transfer to arrange it to their own advantage. See a tax expert if you have enough income and property to benefit from tax games.

f) Income tax

Any income taxes owed or refunds due should be divided with the rest of your property. Most people split these 50-50, but you can agree to any division you want. If you settle division of taxes in a settlement agreement (chapter E), you do not need to list them in your Decree. You also need to decide how to divide any income tax that you *will owe* or refunds you *will receive* for the year of the divorce itself. The easiest way is to agree that each of you will be responsible for taxes incurred on his or her own income only. If your divorce is completed before December 31, you will file taxes as "single" or "head of household."

If you do not have your Decree by December 31, you have the option of filing as "married filing jointly" or "married filing separately." If you and your spouse are in agreement, work up the tax forms both ways to see which form of filing is most advantageous to both of you and share the benefit.

Keep in mind that if you and your spouse owe back taxes, the IRS may still hold you liable even if the debt is assigned to your spouse in your divorce. Tax problems are beyond the scope of this book. You should contact a tax lawyer, CPA, or an enrolled IRS agent before you go to court if you have questions.

4. When property is divided by the court

If there is community property or debts of any significance at the time of your divorce, then it must be properly divided. Property can be divided either by agreement of the spouses, or by the judge according to his or her own standards. There are many advantages to working things out by agreement. These are discussed in section 5 below, but first it might help to understand how things work when left to the court to divide.

The judge has a great deal of discretion, as the law specifies only a division that is "just and right, having regard for the rights of each party and any children." This makes it very important to get an agreement with your spouse, otherwise some stranger (the judge) who knows nothing about you or your family will decide and no one can predict how it will come out. If required to decide at trial, judges tend to look at a variety of factors, including fault in the breakup if fault was alleged. This is unfortunate, as it encourages angry spouses to fight about fault in order to grab for a larger share. Fault aside, a judge will consider the capacities and abilities of the spouses, business opportunities, education, relative physical and financial conditions, obligations, disparity of ages, size of separate estates, and disparity in earning capacity or actual incomes. These factors nicely specify arguments that can come up at trial, but it does not help to predict what a judge will do at the end of the case.

The profound uncertainty and huge expense of taking a case to trial makes it extremely important for you to do everything in your power to negotiate an agreement. If you anticipate any difficulty, be sure to read my book *Make Any Divorce Better*, which gives you many specific steps to take to resolve differences and negotiate an agreement.

Where there is significant property, other than personal possessions, that is not divided by the time the Petition is filed, then *all* the valuable property and debts of the spouses should be listed in the Petition. The Petition should indicate which is community and which is separate property. It is also a very good idea to indicate how the Petitioner wishes the property and debts to be divided.

If there is still no agreement by the time of the hearing, the court has almost complete discretion as to how it will divide your property. This leaves things pretty wide open, so anything can happen. The court is supposed to consider the property, the children, earning ability of each spouse, and any other circumstances the judge thinks relevant, then the judge will make a decision that is difficult to reverse. The judge will be strongly influenced by the Petition and by the words of the Petitioner at the hearing, and very likely will decide as requested. But there is no guarantee. Even attorneys are sometimes surprised by the judge's decision.

The judge will usually divide *only* the community property, and will clarify who owns which items of separate property. However, in rare cases where it seems necessary, the judge may invade a spouse's separate property for the benefit of children.

Here are some general rules of thumb for you to consider, but you must keep in mind that there is no certainty as to what kind of order a judge will make.

a) An approximately equal division of the property and debts will most likely be ordered where there are no children and the spouses have equal earning abilities and equal circumstances. This is especially true in short marriages. Where an item has a debt attached to it—if it was mortgaged or bought on time—the spouse getting the item will most often get the debt too.

b) An unequal division of the property and debts may be ordered in favor of the spouse with:
   - custody of the child(ren)
   - greater need,
   - lesser earning ability, or
   - favorable circumstances of fairness.

c) The judge can, and you should, consider taxes on property and when the tax will have to be paid; say where a spouse gets the house intending to sell it, thus incurring capital gains tax.

Where there are children, the family home and furnishings are almost always kept together for the benefit of the children and awarded to the spouse with custody. The wage-earner spouse may be ordered to pay debts on items he or she does not possess (if he or she fails to pay, the creditor may come and get the stuff anyway).

If the court awards you property that is still in the possession of your spouse, you have to figure out how to get it. If you can't get it peacefully, then you will need an attorney to help you get it, if it is worth the money and trouble.

5. Dividing it by agreement

If your property is minimal, you can just go ahead and divide it up, and that will be that. If there are items of some value, it is usually better to make a written agreement, just to help you keep track of what it was you actually agreed to. If there is any real estate, or if you are dividing a pension plan, then any agreement *must* be in writing.

In uncontested divorces, a judge will almost always follow your agreement, so long as it appears to be generally fair, but the judge is not legally bound to follow your contract. Especially in matters of child custody and support, a judge will want to make sure that your terms are reasonable and fair and children are protected.

Chapter E discusses written agreements and shows you how to make one.

6. How to transfer titles to property

Some property is held under a document or written indicator of ownership, called "title." This includes real estate, motor vehicles, boats, trailers, bank accounts, investment accounts, stocks, and bonds. In such cases, ownership after divorce is not complete until title has been properly transferred or otherwise dealt with.

As with every other part of your divorce, it is always much easier if your spouse will cooperate with you. If this is not possible, you can usually accomplish your goal some other way, but not always. If your spouse is not cooperative, then getting title is merely the first step—you still have to get possession. In some cases, it means a lot to have possession first, as with bank accounts that could be spent while you are waiting around to get title. If you can't get possession in any peaceful way, you may have to seek the help of an attorney.

a) **Real estate** is easy to transfer if your spouse will sign a warranty deed, which is included with the forms in the back of this book. The deed is then recorded at the Clerk's Office in the county where the land is located. There will be a very nominal recording fee of a few dollars. It is very helpful to have this done before the hearing; if possible, even before you file your Petition.

If the transfer is not made by the time you file your Petition, you must list it, being careful to use the exact legal description of the property, which you can copy from your deed, which you can find at the Clerk's Office in the county where the land is located. If the transfer is still not voluntarily made by the time of your hearing, the property must be awarded as part of the Decree. If the land is in Texas, title can be transferred merely by filing a certified copy of the Decree with the Clerk's Office in the county where the land is located. If the land is not in Texas, make sure your Decree specifically orders your spouse to make a transfer by deed to you. Then you have to try to enforce the order by contempt proceedings. This will require the service of an attorney.

b) **Vehicles** can be transferred by a cooperative spouse merely by the signing of the form on the back of the vehicle title slip. You can also have your spouse sign a Power of Attorney to Transfer Motor Vehicle in front of a Notary Public. A copy of the form is in the back of this book. Take this to the auto transfers office in your county within 10 working days of the date of the signature. If the title slip has been lost, you will need to pick up a special form at that office to replace the lost one. If your spouse will *not* cooperate, then the vehicle must be listed and awarded to you in the Decree. The description must be very complete, including make, model, year, license plate number, and motor or vehicle I.D. number. Take a certified copy of the Decree to the auto transfers office and they will have you fill out a couple of forms, pay a few dollars, and the transfer will be made.

Any way you do it, if there is a lien on the auto (where you owe money on it), the lien must be brought forward on the new title.

c) **Bank accounts** are commonly held in one of three ways: (i) in an individual name, (ii) in the names of "H or W," (iii) in the names of "H and W." If the account is in your own individual name, it is yours and you don't have to worry about it. If it is in the individual name of your spouse, then even an attorney would have a hard time doing much about it. The easiest thing to do is to list it on the Petition at its value at that time, and have it awarded to your spouse as a setoff for something else that you want. If the account is in the name of you *or* your spouse, as is most common, this means either one of you can withdraw it at any time. You might want to take out as much as you wish to protect and put it into an account in your own name. Joint accounts in the name of one spouse *and* the other are probably rare. This would mean that the signatures of *both* spouses are required to make a transfer. In such a case, if your spouse will not cooperate, take a certified copy of the divorce Decree to the bank and see if that does the trick. If not, a court order will be required and you will need an attorney's services to get it. Until then, the money is safe, since your spouse can't get it either. Call Divorce Helpline for assistance with this issue.

This discussion applies also to other types of property and instruments, such as stocks and bonds which, like bank accounts, can be held individually or jointly. Possession of the paper means a great deal, especially with "bearer" instruments such as government bonds, which can be negotiated by whoever has possession.

d) Tax refunds are easy with the cooperation of your spouse, and fairly easy in any event if you have possession of the refund check. Either get your spouse's signature when and where required, or take the check along with a certified copy of the divorce Decree to the nearest IRS office. If you do not have possession of the check, then use your innate cunning to get it peacefully, or forget it. A lawyer has a few tricks that sometimes work, but it's rarely worth it, since the check is usually not even big enough to pay the lawyer's fee.

e) Insurance policies can be transferred merely by sending the insurance company a certified copy of the Decree awarding the policy or any covered property to you.

7. Wills, trusts, and beneficiaries

After a divorce, you should definitely make a new will—or better yet, a living trust—and review persons you previously named as beneficiaries in wills, trusts, insurance policies, bank or investment accounts, or named in a pre-divorce Health Care Directive. Call Divorce Helpline and let our attorneys answer questions, give you advice, and assist you with a new will, living trust, or Health Care Directive.

C. Children: Custody and Visitation

1. Generally

When you have children, a divorce never completely ends the relationship. You no longer live together, but chances are you will still be involved because of the children. This makes it extremely important that you try to keep things as calm and pleasant as possible. It is not good for the children or for their parents if you can't get over your differences at least enough to permit the parental relationship to continue and grow.

Managing and Possessory Conservators. Sometimes it's easy to believe that lawmakers have a special department to figure out how to make simple things sound complicated. In Texas, what normal people call custody, the law calls "conservatorship." The parent with custody is the "managing conservator" and the other parent (the one who visits) is the "possessory conservator." What people call "visitation," the law calls "possession." It takes practice, but you will get the hang of it, eventually.

The divorce Petition *must* list all children of the marriage under 18 and not married, including any child natural-born to the spouses or adopted by both. Include stepchildren only if legally adopted by the stepparent. If the wife is pregnant, you have to wait until the child is born to finish your divorce. Any child born to the wife between marriage and divorce is presumed to be her husband's. If this is not the case, you should consult an attorney to help you straighten out the child's paternity.

If custody of any child has come before a court before now, you will need help from an attorney, as the case is now too complicated to do yourself. Call Divorce Helpline for assistance. If you are unsure—if there is even a slight chance that there has been a Texas court involved with the child's custody—you should make a formal inquiry by writing to the Texas Department of Human Resources at 701 W. 51st Street, Austin, TX 78759; give them the full name and birth date of each child and request to know "the court of continuing jurisdiction, if any" for each child listed. If they send back the information that the child is not under the jurisdiction of any court, then you are free to go ahead with your case, but *be sure* you take their response to the hearing with you and put it into evidence.

Modification. Orders about custody, visitation, and support of children are always subject to modification. If circumstances change, either parent can go back into court at any time after one year to seek a change in the court orders.

History of family violence. A history of family violence, abuse or neglect will play a very large role in any judge's determination of custody and visitation (conservatorship and possession), especially if there's evidence of it within the previous two years. If you want restricted visitation, take evidence to your court hearing.

2. Custody (conservatorship)

There are two forms of custody for children in Texas. The law gives preference to *joint managing conservatorship* (JMC), which normal people would call "joint custody." In a JMC, the parents share the duties and responsibilities of raising the child(ren), just like during a marriage. However, those duties and responsibilities are spelled out very specifically in your Decree, so you can tailor your conservatorship to fit the agreement between you and your spouse. JMC does *not* necessarily mean equal or even near-equal periods of custody. It also does not eliminate the requirement for child support. In a joint conservatorship, one parent is selected to provide the primary residence, or domicile, for the child and is called the "home parent."

The second custody form is *sole managing conservatorship*, where one parent is awarded primary custody and responsibilities, while the other parent has more limited duties plus visitation (possession). This used to be the norm, but should now be used only when you can show a judge that joint custody is not in the best interest of your child(ren). Some examples of reasons that sole managing conservatorship might be preferred include: the other parent cannot be located; a parent has a history of substance abuse; the other parent committed family violence against you or the children; or a parent whose physical or mental disabilities could harm the child. Judges may be reluctant to order sole managing conservatorship, so put together strong evidence to bring to court when you have your hearing.

Right now is a good time to go to the back of this book and take a close look at the Conservatorship Order, an Exhibit that goes with the Decree. This form shows you the choices you have to make when you define a child's custody.

Here are some points of law a judge must consider when deciding custody if parents are unable to agree and the matter comes to court:

- Parents are preferred over third parties.
- Joint custody (JMC) is presumed best, but this presumption can be rebutted with evidence. A history of domestic violence removes the presumption.
- The law requires that no preference be given due to marital status or gender of a parent or child. However, for young children there is still a cultural bias in favor of mothers, so if the parents can't agree a father can win custody more easily when the children are older or it is clear that the mother is unfit.

- Split custody (one for me and two for you) is to be avoided.
- Children 12 years of age and older have the right to express a preference to the judge in chambers who he/she wants to live with. The judge can go along with the child's choice, but is not required to. At the judge's discretion, younger children can express a preference in chambers.

If there is a custody battle, in most cases a social study of the family will be ordered. A social worker will be appointed to "study" your family and talk to you and everyone you know and don't know in order to send a report back to the judge, stating facts uncovered and advising what the social worker thinks is best for your child(ren). The lawyers on each side will probably try to make the other side look like a disaster for the kids, and there's even a chance that an older child could end up talking to the judge. Whoever wins, the kids usually lose. Don't do it unless you have no other choice. It is far better to work it out outside of court, if you can do it peacefully. In tough cases, consider using a trusted friend, member of the clergy, mediator, or counselor for help.

You would be foolish to attempt to be your own lawyer if your spouse opposes you legally. Call Divorce Helpline for assistance at (800) 359-7004.

3. Visitation (possession)

Divorce is not the end of the relationship between parents, as there is still the continuing need—duty, in fact—for both to be involved regularly in the lives of their children. Studies have shown that children of divorced parents are most badly damaged when hard feelings and conflict continue long after the divorce, while children adjust fairly nicely if the heat and smoke clear away soon after the Decree. For the sake of your children, make your co-parenting as smooth and comfortable as possible. In conversations with the other parent, talk less about who has custody and more about how you can share the care and parenting of your child(ren).

"Reasonable visitation" is no longer favored because no one knows what it means, so the parents have to constantly work out the details of who has the kids at which times, and this is not easily done when parents are not getting along well. Vast experience has shown that if negotiating a detailed plan is something you can accomplish, parents and children are far better off because everyone will know exactly what the schedule is when the parents can't agree. Parents can arrange visitation any way they like by agreement, without regard for the terms of the Decree, but when relations become strained, the visitation terms define the schedule very clearly, so there's less to argue about.

Standard Possession Order (SPO) and variations

Texas has statewide standard terms for possession—the parenting schedule—that are presumed by law to be in the child's best interest. This is the Standard Possession Order, or SPO, an Exhibit that goes with the Decree. After you finish this section, go to the back of the book and take a close look at the SPO.

If parents can't agree about their parenting schedule and go to court, they'll get the SPO for sure, so why bother? Just do the SPO. On the other hand, if you can agree, you can have almost any reasonable Possession Order you like, so long as you specify which parent has the right to designate the primary residence of the child, either anywhere or within a specific geographical area. In our forms, this is done by reference to the Conservatorship Order, where rights and duties are defined.

The SPO is really for backup, to cover times when you can't agree. You aren't required to be rigid about following the SPO. The very first paragraph says that parents can follow any schedule they like by mutual agreement, otherwise they *must* follow their Possession Order. Ideally, parents will discuss the SPO and decide which responsibilities to share and what schedule is best for their circumstances. Any Possession Order can be changed by mutual agreement or when circumstances change, such as a child growing older.

Joint custody. Where the parents are joint managing conservators (JMC), the SPO is presumed to be the *minimum* amount of possession for the visiting parent, but you can add additional care time to it. Some parents use the Standard Possession Order rigidly, while others prefer to change visits regularly. It is advisable for the children's sake that once you settle on dates and times, you stick to them, as children require stability to feel secure. It would be very unsettling for you not to know until Friday where you were spending the night—think about how your child feels!

Any schedule or written agreement for JMC *must* (1) state which parent has the right to designate the primary residence of the child within a specified geographic area—in our forms, this is done by reference to our Conservatorship Order; (2) specify the rights and duties of each parent, as in our Conservatorship Order form; and (3) include provisions to minimize disruption of the child's education, daily routine, and friendships (what, exactly, this means is not specified, so just use our SPO as a guide).

Variations. Some set of detailed terms *must* be part of any Decree involving custody of children. You can alter the terms of the SPO to fit your work schedules, preferences, or special needs of the parents or child, but there are only two ways to get completely different terms—you can enter into a written agreement with almost any reasonable terms you like, subject to the court's approval; or, without an agreement of the parents, something different from the SPO can be ordered if you can give the court a very good reason for it. If your Possession Order varies more than a little from the SPO in the back of the book and on our CD, remove "Standard" from the Possession Order so the judge will know it is not the standard order.

It is not common, but still possible, that the judge will find your agreement not in the best interest of the children. If this happens, the judge will either issue orders of his own design, or perhaps request a revised agreement.

Children under three. You can create a different schedule for very young children, more suitable for their needs, and provide that they automatically graduate to an attached possession order for older children on their third (or other) birthday.

Virtual visitation means staying in touch with your children via video calls, email, instant messaging, and cell phones. Relatively inexpensive, video calls allow you to hear and see each other, share documents, help with homework, play games, bring friends or grandparents into the visit, and so on. It is not a substitute for quality time spent together, but rather an extremely valuable supplement. Virtual visitation benefits all parties, as it allows the custodial parent to stay in touch with the child during extended summer or holiday visits with the non-custodial parent, and the child never has to feel cut off from either parent at any time. If requested, Texas judges have the discretion to make such orders (Family Code § 153.015). For more information, tales of personal experience, tips on how to do it, and suggestions for virtual visitation language in your settlement agreement, go to **www.internetvisitation.org**.

Visitation problems

Visitation is not tied to support. The parent who has custody is not allowed to forbid visiting because support money is not coming in or because the parents are angry with one another. Visitation is not a weapon to be used against the visiting spouse. But visitation can be refused if it is clear that the child's safety is involved; for example, if the visiting spouse shows up drunk and wants to drive away with the child.

Counties have been authorized since 2001 to set up visitation centers to facilitate visitation or exchange for parents who have (or anticipate) visitation problems. Check with your county to see if they have this service. If they do, pay them a visit to discuss how they can help you.

You should know that there are criminal sanctions against a person who keeps or conceals a child in order to frustrate visitation orders. For example, if the visiting parent just decides to keep the child for awhile and not bring the child home when due, there would be a strong reaction from the authorities if they are called in.

In some very rare cases, it may be clear that it is dangerous for the court to permit any visitation at all. You will have to show the court strong evidence that some specific harm is likely to come to the children if visitation of any kind is allowed. This means clearly showing a pattern of behavior such as heavy use of drugs or alcohol, sexual abuse, or violence toward the children. If you are determined to prevent visitation altogether, you would be better off with an attorney.

4. Class required for parents?

Many counties in Texas now require divorcing parents to take a course on how divorce affects the children and how best to share parenting. These courses are part of a nationwide trend to soften the impact of divorce on children. Both parents must take this course and present proof to the judge at the final hearing. If you do not know where your spouse is, the court may waive the requirement that your spouse attend the class, but you will still have to attend. The course is four hours long and average cost is $30.

Check with the District Clerk's Office in your county to see if you are required to take a parenting course and, if so, get the cost, schedule, location, and other details. Take a look at **www.texasafcc.org/coparent. html** for co-parenting resources, lists of county resources, and other links.

D. Child Support and Alimony

Child Support

Child support services. The Office of the Attorney General, Child Support Division, provides services for parents who wish to obtain or provide support for their children. Their services include (1) locating a noncustodial parent; (2) establishing paternity; (3) establishing and enforcing child support orders; (4) establishing and enforcing medical support orders; (5) reviewing and adjusting child support payments; and (6) collecting and distributing child support payments. If you want to work with a state agency, ask your Clerk's office for more information about these services in your county or look on the Attorney General's web site at **www.oag.state.tx.us**.

Duration. The duty of support lasts until the child marries, dies, becomes self-supporting, begins active service in the U.S. military, or reaches his/her 18th birthday or beyond his/her 18th birthday until high school graduation if the child is enrolled in an accredited secondary school in a program leading toward a high school diploma and complies with the school's attendance requirements. Support can continue indefinitely for a child who is handicapped and unable to provide for him/herself. In any case, unless otherwise agreed in writing or expressly provided in the order, child support terminates on the marriage, emancipation, or death of the child. Support survives the death of the obligor and the unpaid amount due becomes a lump sum charge against the obligor's estate.

Amount set by guidelines. Texas has statewide child support guidelines that judges are required to consider in every case. While not quite mandatory, they are *presumed* to be in the best interest of the child. Without a written agreement with your spouse, if you want to get a different amount ordered, you have to present evidence to show a good reason for departing from the guidelines (section 4 below). Then a judge *may* decide to order a different amount. Here's how the guidelines work:

1. Framework for child support guidelines

a) The guidelines call for the **"obligor"** (the parent who pays) to pay a percentage of his or her **"monthly net resources"** to the **"obligee"** (recipient).

b) The parents can agree to any amount of support, even if it varies from these guidelines, but subject to approval of the court. The court will probably approve any *reasonable* agreement of the parties.

c) On *written* request of either party within *10* days of the child support order, the judge must state the basis for the order, and if the award varied from the guidelines, the reason(s) for the departure *must* be given.

d) The guidelines are applied without regard to gender of the obligor, obligee, or child. In setting child support, the judge may consider the needs of the child, the ability of the parent to contribute to the support of the child, any financial resources available for the support of the child, and the amount of possession of and access to a child by the parties.

2. Figuring obligor's monthly net resources

Step 1. Figure the obligor's total gross annual income and divide by 12 to get a monthly average. "Gross resources" is much broader than the income figure used for tax purposes. It includes all benefits from personal effort—*everything*: (1) all wage and salary income *before* any deductions, and including overtime, commissions, tips, bonuses; (2) interest, dividends, royalties; (3) self-employment income; (4) net rental income (deducting only operating expenses and mortgage payments but not noncash items such as depreciation); and (5) all other income—severance pay, retirement benefits, pensions, trust income, annuities, capital gains, Social Security benefits *other* than supplemental security income, unemployment benefits, disability and worker's compensation, gifts, income from notes, prizes, and spousal maintenance and alimony. Child support actually being received by an obligor (person paying support) is added to the obligor's resources. The only income *not* considered is public assistance received for children, payments for foster care, accounts receivable, and return of principal or capital.

When figuring income from self-employment (includes partnerships, joint ventures, close corporations), include all income and the value of benefits of any kind, allowing deductions only for ordinary expenses and amounts necessary to produce income, but not such things as depreciation, tax credits, or other noncash deductions.

In cases where your spouse is gone, or for any other reason you are unable to get any information about his or her income, the law says wages shall be presumed to be equal to the prevailing federal minimum wage for a 40-hour week. You should go ahead and get your child support order with this figure and when income information becomes available, you will have a basis for filing for modification of child support. When you use this kind of order for a missing spouse, the Attorney General's office can get involved in trying to find the obligor to get the support paid.

Step 2. Subtract allowed deductions. From total resources as defined above, subtract permitted deductions: (1) Social Security taxes; (2) federal income tax based on the tax rate for a single person claiming one personal exemption and the standard deduction; (3) state income tax; (4) union dues; and (5) expenses for health insurance coverage for the obligor's child. If other minors are covered by the same plan, divide the total cost for the insurance by the total number of minors and apply the amount attributed to children of this case. The result after all deductions is the **monthly net resources.**

Tax charts to help you. The Texas Attorney General publishes tax charts for both employed and self-employed people to help you figure net resources once the gross figure is known. Just locate the obligor's monthly gross resources in the left column and the chart gives you the monthly net resources figure. The 2009 charts are on the companion CD in the Forms Etc folder. You can look for updated charts at the web site of the Attorney General: **www.oag.state.tx.us/child/mainchil.shtml**. Unless the obligor lives out of state, the charts do a pretty good job. However, if a significant amount is being paid monthly for health insurance for children, that amount will also have to be deducted to get true net monthly resources.

A judge can also consider any additional factors that increase or decrease the obligor's ability to pay. This includes valuable assets that do not produce an income, income-producing assets that have been voluntarily shifted to produce less income, and income that is significantly less than the obligor could earn because the obligor is voluntarily unemployed or underemployed. The court, in such cases, may apply the guidelines to the earning *potential* of the obligor.

3. Applying the guidelines

The amount of guideline child support is a percentage of obligor's net monthly resources as figured in steps 1 and 2 above. The percentage you apply depends on how many children the obligor and obligee have together and how many other children obligor has by other relationships, as shown in the table below. Here's how you use it.

No other children. Find the number of children you have and look on the first line below that (zero other children) to find the percentage of obligor's net monthly resources that must be paid for child support.

Other children. Use the left column to find the number of children from other relationships that obligor supports and follow that line across to the column under the number of children in the current case. This is the percentage of obligor's net monthly resources that must be paid for child support for the children of *this* case.

		Number of children in this case						
		1	**2**	**3**	**4**	**5**	**6**	**7**
Number of	0	20.00%	25.00%	30.00%	35.00%	40.00%	40.00%	40.00%
other children	1	17.50	22.50	27.38	32.20	37.33	37.71	38.00
obligor has	2	16.00	20.63	25.20	30.33	35.43	36.00	36.44
a legal duty	3	14.75	19.00	24.00	29.00	34.00	34.67	35.20
to support	4	13.60	18.33	23.14	28.00	32.89	33.60	34.18
	5	13.33	17.86	22.50	27.22	32.00	32.73	33.33
	6	13.14	17.50	22.00	26.60	31.27	32.00	32.62
	7	13.00	17.22	21.60	26.09	30.67	31.38	32.00

If the obligor receives Social Security old age benefits, subtract from the guideline support the value of benefits paid to the child through Social Security old age benefits.

Income cap. The court will apply the guidelines to the obligor's first $7,500 of net monthly resources. If there is more, the court can order additional child support as appropriate, depending on the income of the parties and *proven* needs of the child.

Agreements of the spouses will be given great weight and consideration in court, but the judge has the power to make a different order if he/she thinks it is in the best interest of the child. The judge is especially likely to interfere if the support amount seems too low and the custodial parent also has low income.

When hearing your case, the judge is likely to want income tax returns for the past two years and current wage stubs, so take these with you to the hearing. Though not required, it is also a good idea to file or at least take with you a worksheet that shows the income of both spouses and expenses of the custodial parent. We provide a Financial Information worksheet in the forms section at the back of the book and on the CD that you can speak from, show to the judge, or file with the court if you wish.

4. Factors for departing from the guideline

A judge can depart from the guideline only if shown evidence that the guideline amount would be unjust or inappropriate. The judge must consider all relevant factors, including those below. The full list is in Texas Family Code § 154.123, which can be found on the CD, or at **www.capitol.state.tx.us/statutes/fa/fa0015400toc.html**.

    a) the amount of the obligee's net resources, including the earning *potential* if the obligee is intentionally unemployed or underemployed, and any property the obligee may own;

    b) the age and needs of the child;

    c) child care expenses incurred by either party to maintain employment;

    d) whether either party has custody or support of another child, and amounts actually being paid under another child support order;

    e) whether either party has a car, housing, or other benefits furnished by an employer, a business, or another person;

    f) other deductions from wages or other compensation of the parties;

    g) cost of health care insurance and any uninsured medical expenses;

    h) extraordinary educational, health care, or other special expenses of the parties or of the child(ren);

    i) cost of travel to exercise access to or possession of a child;

    j) debts assumed by either party; and

    k) whether Social Security, disability or SSI benefits are received by a party on behalf of the child(ren).

5. Health insurance as additional support

Health care for a child, including dental and vision expenses, is an essential part of the child support obligation, *in addition to* guideline support. The judge *must* see that the child's health care has been provided for and must also consider how accessible the child's health care is from the child's primary residence.

a) If health insurance is available for the child through the obligor's employment or membership in a union, trade association, or other organization at reasonable cost, the court **shall** order the obligor to include the child in the obligor's health insurance.

b) If not available under (a) above, but available through the obligee's employment or membership in a union, trade association, or other organization at reasonable cost, the court **may** order the obligee to provide health insurance for the child and order the obligor to pay additional child support for the actual cost of the health insurance for the child.

c) If not available under (a) or (b) above, the court shall order the obligor to provide health insurance for the child if the court finds that health insurance is available to the obligor from another source at reasonable cost.

d) If neither parent has access to private health insurance at reasonable cost, the court shall order the custodial parent (or, to extent permitted by law, the noncustodial parent) to immediately apply on behalf of the child for participation in whatever public medical assistance program for which the child might be eligible, and that the obligor pay additional child support for the actual cost of such program.

e) If none of the above is available, the court shall order obligor to pay a reasonable amount (as determined by court) each month as medical support.

In the sections above, "reasonable cost" means that the cost of health insurance for all children the payer is required by court order to cover cannot exceed 9% of payer's gross annual income, as defined in section 2, step 1, above.

The court will require the parent ordered to provide health coverage to produce evidence to the court's satisfaction that the parent has applied for and/or secured health insurance, or has otherwise taken action to provide health care coverage, as ordered by the court. A parent ordered to provide health insurance who fails to do so is liable for necessary medical expenses of the child, and the cost of health insurance premiums, if any, paid on behalf of the child.

6. Method of payment and income withholding

Payments to an agency. Judges will almost always order that child support must be paid through either the local registry (in Travis County that is the Domestic Relations

Office and in Williamson County that is the District Clerk's Office) or the State Disbursement Unit (the San Antonio office of the State Attorney General). These registries keep an accounting of payments, so either party can easily show what payments were made. Any payments made not according to the court's order are not counted and are generally considered gifts. The moral of this story: *Don't* make informal payments to the receiving parent and expect to get credit for it!

Income withholding. An order for income withholding is *required* in every case where there is child support. It can also include amounts for spousal maintenance, but only if the recipient has primary custody of the child for whom support is owed and the child resides with him/her. Further, income withholding for spousal maintenance can be ordered if payments are imposed by a court, but there can be no withholding for spousal maintenance agreed by the parties unless the contract specifically permits it, or where payments under a contract have not been made in a timely fashion.

The withholding order remains on file with the court until you ask the clerk's office to "issue" it to the obligor's employer, which usually will cost you about $15. The court retains continuing jurisdiction until all support is paid.

If the obligor is unemployed, self-employed, or can't be located, you obviously need not bother having the order issued until circumstances change. You also have the option of agreeing not to have the order issued as long as support payments do not fall too far behind. In cases where the children are receiving public assistance, the withholding order must be issued.

After support is ordered, it still remains to be collected. Therefore, support in most counties must be paid through the local child support registry or through the Office of the Attorney General. Call the Clerk's office in your county to find out the correct name and address to use in your withholding order, then call that office to ask for an account number. Payment through the registry protects both parents because it gives an unbiased record of payment amounts and dates received. If you are not receiving your child support, the Attorney General's office provides collection services, and larger counties have domestic relations offices that enforce child support for county residents. To enforce child support, tax returns can be intercepted, licenses suspended, wages garnished, and the nonpaying parent can be jailed.

The withholding order requires the name, address, and phone number of the obligor and the obligor's employer, if known; the obligor's Social Security number and driver's license number; and Social Security numbers for the child(ren). Each parent is required to give written notice to the other, to the court, and to the State Case Registry Office 60 days in advance of changes. If you don't know 60 days in advance, you *must* notify the other party within five days of the date you find out. If you have a good reason why you don't want your spouse to know where you are, you do not have to list your own address in public documents.

Life insurance. Parents can agree or the judge can order that the obligor obtain life insurance to secure support in the event of his/her death.

Retroactive child support. The court can make an order for retroactive child support if a petition requesting it is filed not later than the child's 22nd birthday.

Modification. Either party can come back to court any time after one year to modify the support order, where it must be shown that circumstances have changed significantly since the previous order was made. The Attorney General's Office provides a free review of child support for possible modification once every three years, or more often if there has been a change in circumstances. This service may also be available through the Domestic Relations Office in larger counties. Contact these offices for information.

The IRS test for who qualifies to take the dependency exemption depends on who has provided the most financial support. The IRS usually presumes that the "domicile" parent, the one the child lived with most of the year, qualifies to take the exemption. The "non-domicile" parent can claim the exemption only if he or she contributed over half of the child's support *and* the domicile parent agrees to sign IRS Form 8332, which turns over the dependency exemption to the non-domicile parent. In families where the obligor earns a lot more than the obligee, it makes sense to do this, because the family will save on the obligor's taxes and can agree to share the tax savings the obligor realizes. Run the taxes both ways and share the amount saved.

Spousal maintenance (alimony)

Spousal maintenance (alimony) can be ordered for any amount and time period if both parties agree and the support order is incorporated into a written agreement (chapter E), but until 1995, Texas was the only state that had no provision for it by law. Even now, alimony will be required only under very limited circumstances. To be eligible for alimony, a spouse must first show diligence since separation in seeking employment or developing skills to become self-sufficient, though this can be excused where the spouse or a child of the marriage is mentally or physically disabled as defined below. Even then, alimony will be ordered in only two situations:

   a) **Victim of family violence.** Within two years prior to filing the divorce, your spouse was convicted (or received deferred adjudication for) a "family violence offense;" *or*

   b) **Long-term marriages.** You were married at least 10 years and will not have sufficient property after the divorce for your minimum reasonable needs; *and* you (any of the following):

   – Cannot support yourself because you are physically or mentally disabled;

– Have primary conservatorship of a physically or mentally disabled child of the marriage, of any age, who you must stay home to care for; or

– Lack the earning ability to provide for your minimum needs.

"Family violence offense," as used above, means an assault against you, your child, or a family member, or a violation of a family violence protective order. Sometimes criminal mischief (vandalism) or terroristic threats are also considered family violence. If your spouse was convicted of some act and you are not sure it was "family violence," ask the court clerk where the conviction occurred. You will need a certified copy of the conviction to show the judge when you get your divorce.

Amount. A judge can't order monthly maintenance that is more than (a) $2,500 per month, or (b) 20% of the obligor's average monthly gross income, whichever is less. Even then, the judge is to order an amount only sufficient to cover minimum reasonable needs of the obligee, considering employment and property owned after marriage. Gross income for maintenance is the same as "monthly gross resources" for child support (section 2, step 1, above), except that you exclude VA service-related disability compensation, Social Security benefits, disability benefits, and workers' compensation.

Duration. Spousal maintenance cannot last more than three years. This is a very short window of opportunity to upgrade job skills and become employable again. Maintenance ends if you remarry or if you begin cohabiting in a conjugal relationship with another person. If you or a child of the marriage you must stay home to care for are permanently disabled, mentally or physically, you may qualify for indefinite maintenance, subject to review of the court.

Health insurance for spouses

Under federal law (COBRA), spouses and children who will lose their health coverage due to divorce from the primary wage-earner are now entitled to continued coverage and benefits for up to three years at similar rates (100% of what the employer pays), but now at their own expense. The wage-earner may be required to pay for the insurance of the children (see page 63), but the spouse will have to pay for his or her own coverage. To exercise this right, you *must* give written notice of the divorce and your desire to continue coverage to the plan administrator within 60 days after your Decree is signed by the judge. The plan *cannot* insist on new evidence of insurability. Compare rates and coverage available to you under other alternatives before you decide.

If you are presently covered by a health plan provided through *your* employer and it provides coverage comparable to your spouse's plan, your spouse's employer is not required to offer you COBRA coverage. To be sure, contact the plan administrator at your spouse's company. They may want to see a copy of the policy your employer provides to decide whether you qualify for the COBRA option.

E. Marital Settlement Agreements

We have several times discussed the impressive advantages of a divorce by agreement, and now it is at last time to show you how this is actually done.

Marital settlement agreements are subject to the approval of the court. Judges are especially likely to take a close interest in the arrangements you have made for the custody and support of your child(ren), if any. Still, assuming that the agreement appears to be generally fair, it is almost certain that it will be approved.

In matters of child support and custody, the court retains its power to modify its orders no matter what the parties have agreed. This means that in the future, should circumstances change in some important way, either party can come back into court for a different order concerning the best interests of the minor children.

For a marital agreement to be enforceable in the future, it must fulfill two minimum conditions:

- The agreement must be generally fair.
- It must have been made without undue pressure, force, mistake, or fraud. No bullying or cheating, in other words.

We are going to show you two different ways to go about a divorce by agreement. The first is the Approved Decree, and then there is the full-blown marital settlement agreement.

1. The approved Decree

This is an easy way to do an agreed divorce. By this method, you prepare the Decree well ahead of time (chapter 7), and both parties sign their approval of it. Under this method, your property, if there is any, should be itemized in the Petition.

Read the rest of this book until you understand when and how the Decree is used, then prepare a Decree that is agreeable to both you and your spouse. Then, on the last page, at the very bottom, both parties date and sign their approval of the Decree. You will need the original and two copies to take to court and a signed copy for the Respondent to keep. Follow all the other instructions in this book, and when you get to the hearing, present the signed Decree to the judge. Tell the judge you recognize the signature as that of your spouse and that the Decree has been agreed to and approved by both of you. After the hearing, give the Respondent a certified copy of the Decree to show that the agreement was completed.

2. The marital settlement agreement

This kind of agreement is detailed and formal, and takes a bit of effort to work up. If you have a large or intricate estate, use DealMaker software (see inside front cover) instead of this simple agreement. If you have any questions or uncertainty about it and want help, call Divorce Helpline for assistance.

Every situation is different, and therefore every contract should be different. There is no one form that will do in every situation. The contract shown here is included so you can see what one looks like, how it works. You can use it as a guide in preparing your own agreement. Use parts that apply to you and disregard others. Change it to suit your own case, but do not leave out paragraphs VIII, IX, X, or XI.

If you have any trouble at all understanding the contract or wording it to fit your situation, do not attempt to do it yourself. Use DealMaker software or get help. Call Divorce Helpline or see chapter A, section 11 for other options.

Joint custody (Joint Managing Conservatorship). A written agreement for JMC *must* (1) state which parent has the right to designate the primary residence of the child within a specified geographic area, as we do in our Conservatorship Order; (2) specify the rights and duties of each parent, as we do in our Conservatorship Order form; and (3) include provisions to minimize disruption of the child's education, daily routine and friendships (what, exactly, this means is not specified, so just use our Standard Possession Order as a guide).

If you decide to make your own contract, study the Decree first and see if there are any terms in the Decree that you want to include in your agreement. When done, make an original, a copy for your spouse, and three copies to take to the hearing with you. Get it signed before you go to court, of course.

The contract has the same caption as the other forms because it gets filed and becomes an official court document. Mark one of the copies "Exhibit A" (or some other number if there are other Exhibits attached) and attach it to your Decree so the agreement is properly before the Court.

For your convenience, the agreement in this chapter is also found in the MSA folder on our companion CD so you can edit it to make your own agreement.

Cause No._____

In the Matter of the Marriage of:

_____ Petitioner

and

In the District Court

of _____ County

_____ Respondent

_____ Judicial District

And in the Interest of

_____

_____ Child(ren)

Marital Settlement Contract

I,   , Husband,

and I,   , Wife, agree as follows:

I. GENERALLY: We are now husband and wife. We were married on   , and separated on   . We make this agreement with reference to the following facts:

    A. Children: There are

        a) no children, and none are expected.

        b) the following minor children of the parties
           (*list by full name and give sex and birth date for each child*).

    B. Our marriage has become insupportable because of discord or conflict of personalities such that there is no reasonable expectation for reconciliation. For this reason, we now desire to settle our mutual rights and duties as set forth below.

II. SEPARATION: We agree to live separately and apart, and, except for the duties and obligations imposed and assumed under this agreement, each shall be free from interference and control of the other as fully as if he or she were single. We each agree not to molest, interfere with, or harass the other.

III. CUSTODY OF CHILDREN: The (Wife/Husband) shall be the Managing Conservator of the child(ren), to have full parental rights, duties, and powers, subject only to the rights of the (Husband/Wife), as Possessory Conservator, to visit with and temporarily take possession of the child(ren) as follows: (specify)

(see chapter C, section 3 and the Schedule for Possession in Forms section)

IV. SUPPORT OF CHILDREN: Subject to the power of the court to modify these terms, (Husband/Wife) shall pay to (Wife/Husband), as and for child support, the sum of $ per (wk./mo.), beginning on the   day of   , 20   , and continuing until the first to occur of the following: the child reaches the age of 18, except that if the child is fully enrolled in an accredited program leading to a high school degree and the child complies with the attendance requirements of the school, then child support shall continue until the end of the month in which the child graduates; the child marries; the child dies; the child becomes self-supporting; enlists in the U.S. armed forces or is otherwise emancipated.

(If there is more than one child, repeat the next sentence as many times as necessary until only one child is left to support. The amount paid after each reduction of support must equal or exceed the child support guidelines for the number of children still being supported.)

Thereafter, (Husband/Wife) shall pay to (Wife/Husband) as and for child support the sum of $ per (wk/mo.) beginning on the   (same as above) day of the first month following the occurrence of any of the above described events.

This obligation shall survive the death of the obligor. This obligation shall cease if obligor becomes the Managing Conservator.

If there is a handicapped child, add this: Support for (*name of child*) shall continue beyond the age of eighteen, as said child requires continuous care and personal supervision and is unlikely to become self-supporting.

Optional terms:

In addition, during the term of the support obligation for the child(ren), (Husband/Wife) shall

a) carry and maintain life insurance in the amount of $, naming the child(ren) as beneficiary(ies).

b) carry and maintain medical and hospital insurance for the child(ren)'s benefit.

c) pay for (required/extraordinary) medical and dental expenses.

V. PAYMENTS TO SPOUSE: In order to fully discharge all obligations arising from the marriage, other than division of property, (Husband/Wife) agrees to pay to (Wife/Husband) the sum of $ per month, payable on the   day of each month, beginning on   , 20   , and continuing until:

a) the death of (you can name one or both parties)

b) the remarriage of the recipient

c) some other date or condition

These spousal maintenance payments __ may be __ may not be the subject of an income withholding order.

VI. DIVISION OF PROPERTY AND DEBTS:

A. Property Transferred to Wife: Husband transfers and quitclaims to Wife as her sole and separate property the following items: (list—include items that are already Wife's separate property).

B. Property Transferred to Husband: Wife transfers and quitclaims to Husband as his sole and separate property the following items: (list—include items that are already Husband's separate property).

Note: If there is a community interest in a pension plan, be sure to list and dispose of it in this section.

Note: Here is an alternative way to deal with property for small estates: Husband and Wife agree that they have already divided the property to their mutual satisfaction, and each hereby transfers and quitclaims to the other any and all interest in any property in the possession of the other, and agrees that whatever property the other may possess is now the sole and separate property of the other.

C. Insurance: Wife (or Husband) is expressly retained as the beneficiary of the following insurance policies: (description)—or—Wife (or Husband) is no longer the beneficiary of any insurance policy carried by Husband (or Wife).

D. Debts Assumed by Husband: Husband shall pay and hold Wife harmless from the following debts: (*list and give specific description of each one*).

E. Debts Assumed by Wife: Wife shall pay and hold Husband harmless from the following debts: (*list and give specific description of each one*).

VII. TAXES: The parties agree that:

Any tax refunds for the current tax year will be distributed as follows: (*specify*).

Any tax deficiencies for the current tax year shall be paid as follows: (*specify*).

VIII. EXECUTION OF INSTRUMENTS: Each party agrees to execute and deliver any documents, make all endorsements, and do all acts that are necessary or convenient to carry out the terms of this agreement.

IX. APPROVAL BY COURT: At the divorce proceeding, this agreement shall be presented to the court for incorporation into the Decree, and the parties shall, by the terms of the Decree, be ordered to comply with all terms of this agreement.

X. DISCLOSURES: Each party has made a full disclosure to the other of his or her current assets and income, and each enters into this agreement in reliance thereupon.

XI. BINDING EFFECT: This agreement, and each provision of it, is expressly made binding upon the heirs, assigns, executors, administrators, representatives, and successors in interest of each party.

Dated: _____   _____
                                                        Husband

Dated: _____   _____
                                                        Wife

Part Two

How to Do Your Own Divorce

WE CAN DO IT FOR YOU

You probably have important things to do with your time, so if your plate is already full, let us take this red-tape burden off your hands. You will feel better knowing that your paperwork will be done promptly and correctly by Divorce Helpline's staff of family law attorneys and documents experts, supervised by Texas attorney Bruce Naraghi.

 (800) 359-7004

1. Introducing the Forms

In the back of this book you will find a complete set of forms for doing your own uncontested divorce. The same forms, plus several others, are on the companion CD, for use on a Windows or Mac computer. These are the basic forms you will use:

In every case

The Petition states basic information about your marriage and tells the court what you want. When your spouse gets a copy, it will give notice of what you intend to ask for in court. Next, you will use either the Citation or the Waiver, but not both.

The Citation is a message from the court to your spouse, commanding an answer to the Petition within 20 days. It also contains a form where the officer serving the papers signs the details of the service. Instead of the Citation, you can use the Waiver.

The Waiver is the statement of a cooperative spouse that the Petition was received and giving permission for the matter to proceed without contest.

The Decree and attached Exhibits contain the findings of fact and orders of the court dissolving your marriage and detailing the terms of the divorce.

Cases with children

The Child Information form adds required information to your Petition.

The Standard Possession Order goes with the Decree and sets out detailed terms for possession (visitation) of the children.

The Order/Notice to Withhold Income for Child Support is used in every case where child support is ordered. If it is served on the paying spouse's employer, it requires that sums be taken from wages and paid into an office of the court, then promptly remitted to the person caring for the children.

The Request to Issue Withholding Order is a request to the clerk to have the withholding order served on a specific employer so that it can go into effect.

Other useful forms

Both the book and CD contain additional forms that will be useful to some people, including a property checklist, an information sheet for the officer serving the Citation, kits for publication of the Citation, detailed health insurance order attachments to the Decree, property and debt order attachments, a financial information form to take to the hearing, an employer's order for alimony, power of attorney to transfer title to a vehicle, and a warranty deed to transfer title to real estate.

2. Checklists

A. Preplanning Checklist

Once you have decided definitely to get a divorce, and after you have decided to do it yourself, you then have to plan out just how you are going to go about doing it:

1. Divorce by agreement or by default?

It is much easier and better if you can divorce by agreement, but much more common for it to be done by default. Carefully review chapters A, sections 5 and 9; and chapter E. Try to work toward an agreed divorce, but if it cannot be done, or if you do not want to try, proceed by default.

2. Decisions that must be made

    a) how to divide the property (chapter B), *and*

    b) arrangements for child custody, visitation, and support (chapters C and D).

3. Plan how to give notice to your spouse:

If you can proceed by agreement, you will undoubtedly have your spouse sign the Waiver form.

    If you proceed by default, you must consider how notice can be delivered to your spouse. If there is any chance that your spouse will try to evade service, you have to plan the best way to get through (chapter 6). If your spouse cannot be found, you will have to publish the Citation (forms for this are found on the companion CD or at **www.nolodivorce.com/TX**.

The Agreed Divorce

At a minimum, Respondent will sign the Waiver permitting the case to be completed without his/her further participation. Ideally, if you have children or property or debts to divide, you will also have a written marital settlement agreement.

B. Checklist for the Agreed Divorce

1. If you have children, real estate, a lot of property, or the desire to be perfectly clear and secure, you should have a written agreement. Review chapter E, decide whether to use the approved Decree or a contract, then prepare the forms you and your spouse decide to use.

2. Prepare the Petition (chapter 5). If you have children, you might also need to attach the Child Information form. In Travis County, you must also attach the Travis Standing Orders form (on CD or get from court).

3. File the Petition and pay the filing fee with cash or a money order (chapter 4).

4. Prepare: the Waiver (chapter 6, section A)
   the Decree and necessary Exhibits (chapter 7)
   Exhibit 6 - Required Information
   the Statistics form (chapter 8)

   If you have property or debts to divide, also prepare:
   Exhibit 7 - Orders Re Property and Debts

   If you have children, ask the Clerk if you and your spouse must attend a parenting class, then prepare:
   Exhibits 2–5 concerning children
   the Order/Notice to Withhold Earnings, and maybe
   the Request to Issue Withholding Order (chapter 9)

   Optional, but recommended when child support is requested:
   the Financial Information form (in back of book)

   If you have alimony, also prepare the Employer's Notice to Withhold Earnings (chapter 9).

5. Have your spouse sign the Waiver before a notary and any written settlement agreement you have agreed to use.

6. File the Waiver.

7. Choose a date and go to the Hearing (chapter 11).

The Default Divorce

Respondent was properly served (chapter 6) but filed no documents with the court: no Answer, no Waiver; nothing.

C. Checklist for the Default Divorce

1. Prepare the Petition (chapter 5). If you have children, you might also need to attach the Child Information form. In Travis County, you must also attach the Travis Standing Orders form (on CD or get from court).

2. File the Petition (chapter 4) and pay the filing fee with cash or a money order.

3. Arrange for the Citation to be served on your spouse. In a few counties, you may have to prepare the Citation yourself (chapter 6, section B).

4. Prepare: the Decree and necessary Exhibits (chapter 7)
   > Exhibit 6 - Required Information
   > the Statistics form (chapter 8)
   > the Military Affidavit (chapter 11)

   If you have property or debts to divide, also prepare:
   > Exhibit 7 - Orders Re Property and Debts

   If you have children, ask the Clerk if you and your spouse must attend a parenting class, then prepare:
   > Exhibits 2–5 concerning children
   > the Order/Notice to Withhold Earnings, and maybe
   > the Request to Issue Withholding Order (chapter 9)

   > Optional, but recommended when child support is requested:
   > the Financial Information form (in back of book)

   If you have alimony, also prepare the Employer's Notice to Withhold Earnings (chapter 9).

5. Choose a date and go to the Hearing (chapter 11)

3. How to Use the Forms

This book contains paper forms in the back and computer forms on the companion CD. They are complete and completely legal and they will work for you. The computer forms have a slight advantage in that, after you edit them to suit your case, they will look just like forms attorneys file, whereas with the paper forms, you have to cross out parts you don't use. No real problem; they've been working fine since 1980.

There is no legal requirement that court documents be in any particular size, shape, or style. The only requirement stated in the law is that they be in writing, and even that rule has exceptions. However, what attorneys almost always submit, and what judges are used to and expect, are documents that are typed on 8.5 x 11-inch paper.

There is some advantage to having your papers look like all the others the judge is used to seeing. Texans file 85,000 to 100,000 divorces each year, so Texas judges are buried to their ears in divorce cases. They do not have the time or desire to give special attention to any one case if they can help it. Clerks might go over cases of people representing themselves to make sure everything is in order, or at the hearing the judge may ask you some questions to make sure you know what you are doing and look to see that your paperwork checks out. If any of your requests are unusual (giving custody of a child to a non-parent, or asking to change the husband's name to Florence, or taking $250 for support from a person who makes $100,000), then you are inviting some extra questions and explanations. It always goes much easier when your case is pretty much like all the others before and after it.

There are *three* ways you can use the forms in this book:

- **Use the computer forms** that come on the companion CD that comes with this book and edit and print them yourself. Use our language and format, but delete the check boxes and all parts that don't apply to your case. This will give you clean copy and your forms will look much like all the others on the judge's bench. Computer forms can be purchased or downloaded at **www. nolodivorce.com/TX**.

- **Printed forms** that come with this book are the easiest and cheapest thing for you to prepare, and, like we said, they will work just fine. If for any reason you want an extra set of blank forms, you can either print them from the forms on the CD, or order a set of paper forms by calling Nolo, or order from our web site at **www.nolodivorce.com/TX**, or via mail with the order form in the back.

- **Custom-typed forms** can be made up by you or by a typist, using our forms as your guide.

A. General instructions

These instructions show you how to use the forms that come with this book. Whether you decide to edit and print your own forms or have them done for you by a typist, you should still make up one set of forms as shown here to use as your worksheets. It will help eliminate errors.

1. Keep all papers and receipts orderly, neat, and in one safe place.

2. **Computer forms.** Use any word processor to edit the forms provided on the CD. Computers may handle fonts and pages differently, so if any form looks awkward or shows unfortunate page breaks, edit the form to make it tidy. Use only portions that are required by your case, delete check boxes and all text that does not apply to you, and if entire items are deleted, re-number items that follow. Correct page numbers at the bottom if necessary. A lazy option would be to print the forms as they appear and simply use them like the paper forms.

3. **Paper forms.** Make high-quality copies of the blank forms in the back of this book, so you will have extras in case you make a mistake. Prepare your final version on good copies so they will be a full 8.5 x 11 with no ragged left edge. Use a typewriter to fill in the blanks in the forms as shown by the instructions. It is not illegal for you to hand print in ink, but typed forms are preferred. Whatever parts do not apply to your case should be crossed out by drawing heavy lines through them in ink. Use a ruler to make straight lines.

4. On documents with more than one page, if not already present, type in page numbers at the bottom of each page, like this: "1 of 3," "2 of 3," "3 of 3." The last number is the total number of pages of that document, not including any attachments.

5. When your forms are accurate and complete, make four high-quality copies of each one. You need only two, but it will be convenient to have more and it doesn't cost much.

Notarizing documents

At least two documents you are likely to use will need to be notarized when signed, including the Waiver of Citation, which is commonly used and very important. A Notary Public can be located in the yellow pages or at most banks; call around.

Military Personnel. Military people on duty overseas will probably not be able to find a Notary, but they can have documents notarized by any of the many officers in their command structure who have been given notary powers.

B. The caption

At the top of each legal document is a heading, called a caption, which is filled out like this:

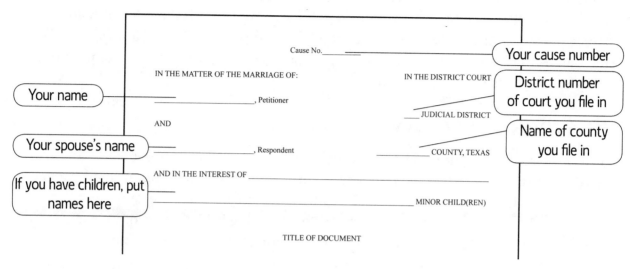

The Cause Number (case number) and the Judicial District Number (number of your court) are assigned when you file the Petition, and after that must be filled in on any document you file. The Court Number identifies your court, the one that will be handling and hearing your case. The Cause Number is their identification for your file and case.

If there are children of this marriage, they must be named in the caption; otherwise that part of the caption is crossed out or left off. Include any legally adopted children. If the wife is pregnant, do not start your own divorce until the child is born.

C. Petitioner/Respondent

The Petitioner is the spouse who files the papers and goes to court. The Respondent is the other spouse. Apart from possibly signing a Waiver and/or written agreement, the Respondent does nothing—files no papers, does not go to court.

D. Pro Se

This term appears in a few places on the forms and you may hear it in court. It is a legal Latin term meaning "for self," which indicates that you are appearing as your own attorney.

E. Names

Use the full legal names of parties and children. You must be consistent, so names will appear exactly the same way each time, including signatures. The court will not know, for instance, that John Smith, J. W. Smith, John W. Smith, and J. Wilson Smith are different names for the same person. It is good form to type the names in capitals. Use the names in normal order—last names go last. Use the wife's married name unless the form requests her maiden name.

F. Protecting privacy

You can omit private information in cases where you can show a reasonable concern for the safety of yourself or a child. Simply omit any of the following from all papers filed in your divorce: the child's sex, place of birth, place of residence, and the parents' ages and places of residence. At your hearing, the judge is likely to require some factual evidence, at least your testimony, to show your concern is reasonable.

Sealing documents. In order to protect the parties and children from the threat of identity theft, in your Petition you can ask the judge to seal from public view the attachments to the Decree that contain identifying information. It is entirely up to the judge's discretion whether to grant this request, as it is not mandated by law.

G. Copies

Type each form neatly, check for errors, then make four copies of each page on a high-quality copy machine. When there is more than one page to a document, staple the pages together in the upper left-hand corner.

The court always gets the original of each form, the Respondent gets a copy, and you keep a copy for your files. Thus you need an original and two copies of each document, but you should make two extra copies in case you want them later. It is an especially good idea to have extra copies of the Decree. When you file the Decree, have the clerk certify your copies, and keep them for future use.

4. How to File Your Papers

Filing papers is easy. Just take them to the District Clerk's Office and hand them to the clerk. When you file the Petition, you must also pay the filing fee. You could mail them in with a self-addressed stamped envelope, but doing it in person saves you wondering if they got there, if they are acceptable, and when they are coming back.

The county in which you file your papers is determined by which spouse satisfies residency requirements (chapter A, section 3c) and is usually the one you live in, but it could be the one Respondent lives in. Papers are filed at the District Clerk's Office in that county. You will want to get the address and phone number for your court.

Locating your court: If you have access to the Internet, you should look to find out if your county and your court have a web site. If so, you will at least find the address and phone number there, but possibly they will also post important information like local forms and rules that you will want to know about. Start by looking on our companion CD, where we keep a list of counties, links to web sites, and a listing of District Courts sorted by telephone area code and by their district numbers. Finally, you can look in the phone book and call them. The number will be listed under the name of your county, or under "Government." Do not confuse the court with the County Clerk's Office, which is a different thing altogether.

Filing: When you file your Petition, the clerk will give you a Cause Number and assign your case to a court by filling in the number of the Judicial District in your caption. From this time on, all documents must have your cause number on them.

Fees: When you have the District Clerk's Office on the phone, ask how much the filing fee will be. Fees depend on whether there are children and whether Respondent will sign a Waiver or if a Citation will have to be issued. Tell the clerk you want to know the filing fee for a divorce petition, with or without children, and whether there will be a Waiver or if instead you want an in-county or an out-of-county Citation.

Fees must be paid by cash, money order, or cashier's check made payable to "District Clerk, (name of county), Texas." Be sure to get a receipt and keep it in your file. *If you can't afford the fees,* you can file an Affidavit of Inability to Pay—a sworn statement about your finances—and the fees might be waived. See Appendix A.

If your case will not have a Waiver signed by Respondent, a Citation will have to be prepared, issued by the clerk, and forwarded to an officer for service. In most counties, the District Clerk's Office does this for you on their own forms, but some do not. When you have the clerk on the phone, ask whether or not they prepare the Citation, or if it is prepared by the Petitioner. Ask if they forward the Citation for service.

The clerks will not be willing to give you legal advice because they are not attorneys and it would be against the law for them to do so. But if they wish to, they can be very helpful with matters related to the filing of papers and how procedures are handled in their office. Don't be afraid to ask questions. You should also remember that most employees of the District Clerk's offices are (or feel they are) overworked and underpaid. A big smile and politeness on your part can go a long way toward getting your questions answered.

5. The Petition

What it is

The Petition states basic information about your marriage and tells the court what you want done. When it is served on the Respondent, it gives notice of what is happening in court. If the Respondent declines to respond, then the judge is free to assume that all the facts stated in it are true, and the Petitioner's requests are very likely to be granted.

How to fill it out

Fill out the Petition as shown in the illustrations on the next pages.

Then what?

When the forms are completed, check them for accuracy. Make four copies and take the original and all copies to the District Clerk's Office with the filing fee (cash or money order, no personal checks). The clerk will assign a cause number and court number at this time. If you are using the Citation and service method to give notice to your spouse, then take along whatever papers you need for this purpose (chapter 6).

Child support pending in another court?

If you had a child support case pending in another court before filing your divorce, you will want to file a motion to consolidate the two cases into one action. Documents and instructions for doing this can be found in the Forms Etc folder on the CD that comes with this book.

Filing an amended petition

If you later find you made a mistake or left something out, you can file a new Petition so long as the Decree hasn't been filed, only this time you title it "First Amended Petition for Divorce." You won't have to pay another original filing fee, but follow all the same instructions as if you were starting over again, because that is exactly what you are doing, so serve the First Amended Petition and follow your checklist in Chapter 2.

Notes for the first page

Note 1, Caption. The Cause Number and Court Number are left blank. They are assigned by the clerk when you file the Petition. We are told that some counties word this block a little differently—such as *COUNTY COURT AT LAW, NO. ____.* Call your County Clerk to ask how they want this caption worded.

Note 2, Children and the caption. If you have children, you must name them in the caption, but remember that you should include only children born to or adopted by you and your spouse. Do not include stepchildren who have not been legally adopted by the stepparent. If the wife is pregnant, do not do your own divorce until the child is born.

Note 3, Parties. For both parties, use *street* address, not just a post office box.

Note 4, Privacy. In cases where there is some credible threat such that you need to protect the location of a party or a child, you can omit any of the following from all papers filed in your divorce: the child's sex, place of birth, and place of residence; and the parents' ages and places of residence.

Note 5, Discovery level. Read the two paragraphs carefully and check the one that best describes your case. If you have children, you must choose Level 2. Don't worry about it; this is a purely technical requirement, meant more for contested cases that are handled by attorneys.

How to fill out the Petition

First page

Leave blank

Your name

Your spouse's name

If you have children, put names here, otherwise cross this part out.

Leave blank

Leave blank

Name of the county you file in

Your name and address. See note 4.

Your spouse's name and address

Choose one. See note 5 on previous page.

Check one or both boxes to show who meets the residency requirement.

Cause Number _____

IN THE MATTER OF THE MARRIAGE OF: IN THE DISTRICT COURT

_____, Petitioner

AND   ____ JUDICIAL DISTRICT

_____, Respondent   COUNTY, TEXAS

AND IN THE INTEREST OF _____

_____ MINOR CHILD(REN)

ORIGINAL PETITION FOR DIVORCE

1.   **Parties and Discovery**
     This suit is brought by Petitioner, _____, who resides at
     _____

     Respondent is _____, who resides at
     _____

     ☐ Discovery Level 1 applies to this case as there are no minor children of the marriage whose custody and support will be determined, the wife is not pregnant, **and** the value of the marital estate that we currently own is not more than $50,000.00.

     ☐ Discovery Level 2 applies to this case because ☐ there are minor children of the marriage whose custody and support will be determined and/or ☐ the value of the marital estate that we currently own is more than $50,000.00.

2.   **Residency (Domicile)**
     ☐ Petitioner ☐ Respondent has been a domiciliary of the State of Texas for the preceding six months and a resident of the county in which this petition is filed for the preceding ninety days.

Original Petition for Divorce   Page 1 of 7

Notes for the second page

Note 1, Service of Process. Indicate if there will be a Waiver or service of Citation, enter a complete residence address, and add the employment address if you know it.

Note 2, Protective Orders. If you don't have a protective order in effect or pending, cross out all but the first line. If you do have one, fill in the details and attach copies of any order if there is one.

Note 3, Common-Law Marriage. You must file for divorce within two years of separation if your marriage is common-law. If you wait longer, it is presumed that the marriage never existed, and you can't go through a regular divorce. In cases like this you will have to find another way to divide property and establish paternity of children born during the relationship in order to collect support and arrange for visitation.

Note 4, Community Property. Review chapter B carefully, especially section 3, and chapter E. If you and your spouse are in agreement but haven't worked out the details, you can use the second paragraph and cross out the others, but don't use this option unless you are absolutely sure you will get the agreement; you can always bring in an agreement later if you get one. Use the fourth paragraph under item 7 (on page 3) if you have no certain agreement and want the court to be able to make orders about community property. Itemize your property on page 3 as shown below. If there is not enough room for your entire list, don't put any of it on the form—just type in:

> "As listed on attached sheet entitled 'Property List,'
> which is incorporated here by reference."

Then, on a blank sheet, type the heading "Property List" and make your list as shown below. Staple it to the Petition.

Number each item or group of items. It is best, though not required, to give the approximate market values (what you could get if you tried to sell at this time).

You should *list separately:*

- Any item that has special importance to you,
- Any property with documentary title (real estate, bank accounts, vehicles, pension plans, insurance policies with cash surrender value, stocks, etc.),
- Property that is encumbered by debt, together with to whom owed, amount due, and repayment schedule.

All other property can be grouped under general headings.

An example of how to list property is shown below.

How to fill out the Petition

Second page

Cross out parts that do not apply to your case

> Use this part if your spouse will sign the waiver.

> Use this part for all other cases. See Note 1.

3. **Service of Process**

☒ **Waiver.** No service is necessary at this time because Respondent has signed or will sign a Waiver of Service. If my spouse does not sign a Waiver of Service, I will ask a sheriff or constable to give a copy of this Original Petition for Divorce to Respondent at the following address:

_____

☒ Process should be served on Respondent at the following address:

_____

> See Note 2 about protective orders.

4. **Protective Order Statement**

☒ There is no protective order between the parties and no application for one is pending.

☒ A protective order is presently in effect or an application for protective order is pending at this time in the _____ Court, _____ County, Texas, Cause No. _____.
A true and correct copy of the protective order
  ☐ is attached to this Original Petition.
  ☐ is unavailable now but will be filed with the court before any hearings in this case.

5. **Marriage and Separation**

☒ Petitioner and Respondent were married on or about _____, ____, and ceased to live together as husband and wife on or about _____, ____.

☒ Common-Law Marriage: Petitioner and Respondent agreed to be married on or about _____, ____, and thereafter lived together in Texas as husband and wife and there represented to others that they were married, thus creating a common-law marriage. The parties separated on or about _____, ____.

> Use this part for all cases unless you had a common-law marriage.

> Use this part if you had a common-law marriage. See Note 3.

6. **Grounds**

The marriage has become insupportable because of discord or conflict of personalities that destroys the legitimate ends of the marriage relationship and prevents any reasonable expectation of reconciliation.

> Use this part if there is no separate or community property to be divided by the court.

> Use this part if you expect an agreed divorce.

> Use this part if you already have a written settlement agreement.

7. **Community Property (including debts)** (Check only one box)

☒ **No property.** To Petitioner's knowledge, other than personal effects there is no community property of any significant value which is subject to division by the Court at this time.

☒ **Divided by agreement.** Petitioner believes the parties will reach an agreed property division and ask the Court to approve that agreement when presented to the Court or, absent agreement, divide the assets and debts of the parties according to Texas law.

☒ **Marital Settlement Agreement.** The parties have entered into a Marital Settlement Agreement, a copy of which is attached and incorporated by reference.

Original Petition for Divorce   Page 2 of 7

Notes for the third page

Note 1, Divided by Court. If you claimed on page 2 that there is no community property or if you indicated that there is or will be a written agreement, then you do *not* list property or use anything on this page. Cross it all out.

However, unless you have no marital property to divide or are certain you will get an agreement about it, check this box (Divided by Court) and list your community property and debts so the judge will be able to divide them at the hearing.

Note 2, List of Community Property. There are many ways you could list your community property, but we suggest you do it something like this:

1. Personal effects of the Petitioner $465

   Personal effects of the Respondent 875
   (covers clothing, ordinary jewelry, hair brushes, etc.)

2. Sable stole 650

3. Household goods, furnishings, appliances 1,200

4. 1958 Edsel, license no. HOG 101, vehicle I.D. No. 24564R556,
   encumbered by debt to Good Guy Finance Co. in amount
   of $853, payable $75 per month 1,400

5. Ameritrade acct. # 34-5678, 22 shares of XYZ 1,350

6. The Respondent's vested retirement account, Teacher's Union
   Retirement Account no. 76R456 8,000

7. House and lot located at 10 Downing Street, Clyde, Texas, described
   as Lot 1, Section 3, on Map 33, Page 4, Plat Records, Cork County,
   Texas, encumbered by:

   Mortgage, loan no. 54-56-78900, Lubbock First National
   Bank, Lubbock, Texas in the amount of approximately $33,654,
   payable at $144 per month 40,500

Note 3, Debts. Any debt not already listed as secured by some property item should be listed separately, together with a word or two about what it's for, the amount, payment schedule, and to whom owed. For example:

Debts:

8. Home Finance Co., for dental work, $75 per month $839

9. J. Jones, Respondent's father, for vacation, no fixed
   schedule of payments 950

Notice that the item numbers run consecutively through the entire list.

How to fill out the Petition

Third page

Cross out parts that do not apply to your case

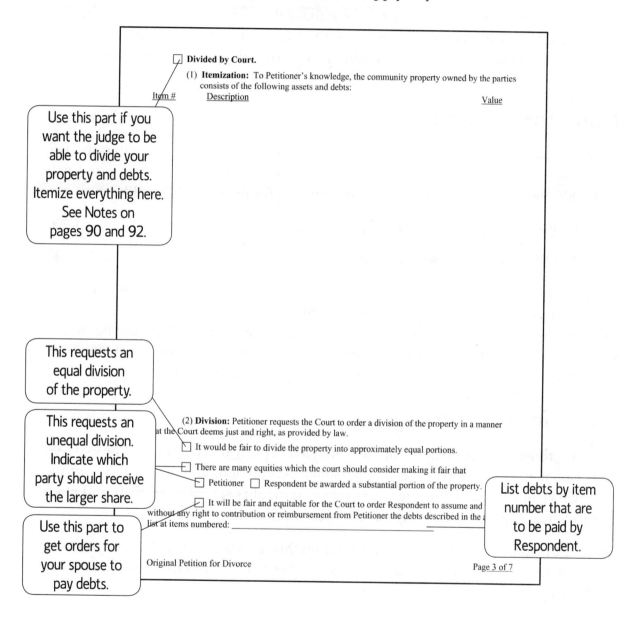

☐ **Divided by Court.**

(1) **Itemization:** To Petitioner's knowledge, the community property owned by the parties consists of the following assets and debts:

Item #   Description   Value

Use this part if you want the judge to be able to divide your property and debts. Itemize everything here. See Notes on pages 90 and 92.

This requests an equal division of the property.

This requests an unequal division. Indicate which party should receive the larger share.

Use this part to get orders for your spouse to pay debts.

(2) **Division:** Petitioner requests the Court to order a division of the property in a manner at the Court deems just and right, as provided by law.

☐ It would be fair to divide the property into approximately equal portions.

☐ There are many equities which the court should consider making it fair that

☐ Petitioner ☐ Respondent be awarded a substantial portion of the property.

☑ It will be fair and equitable for the Court to order Respondent to assume and without any right to contribution or reimbursement from Petitioner the debts described in the list at items numbered: _____

List debts by item number that are to be paid by Respondent.

Original Petition for Divorce   Page 3 of 7

Notes for the third page (continued)

Note 4, Division. Unless you show up in court with a written agreement, the judge will look into your community assets and debts and divide them. The paragraphs under the property list are your requests stating how you wish to have things divided. It is not required that you make any requests about the division of property; you *could* cross out all requests, leaving the matter up to the court to decide. However, judges prefer you to indicate ahead of time how you would like property and debts to be divided. It makes their job, and yours, much easier at the hearing.

Notes for the fourth page

Note 1, Separate Property. If there is any separate property belonging to either spouse, especially items of value or special importance, it should be listed at item 8 and valued. This makes everything very clear for now and for the future. Do it like this:

1. Family heirloom gold chain.. $1,200

2. Oil paintings of a seascape and a cucumber 45

Note 2, Spousal Maintenance. If you do not want maintenance (alimony) or if you have already arranged for it in a Marital Settlement Contract, cross out everything after the first sentence. If you request alimony, choose whether you are asking for alimony based on a 10-year marriage or on a family violence occurrence or both. Then choose which of the three additional grounds applies and cross out the others.

Notes for the fifth page

Note 1, Privacy. In cases where you can show that a party or a child might be exposed to harassment or abuse by revealing personal information, you can omit any of the following from all papers filed in your divorce: the child's sex, place of birth, and place of residence; and the parents' ages and places of residence.

Note 2, Children. If there are no children from this marriage (either born to you both or adopted), use the first sentence and cross out the rest of item 11, otherwise fill it out as shown in the illustration.

Note 3, Husband not bio-dad. If a child born during marriage is not the biological child of the husband, list any such child here.

Note 4, Child Information form. If you have children and either parent resides outside of Texas, you must attach the Child Information form (illustrated at the end of this chapter). If you can show that revealing personal information might endanger a party or child, this form can be omitted.

How to fill out the Petition

Fourth page

Cross out parts that do not apply to your case

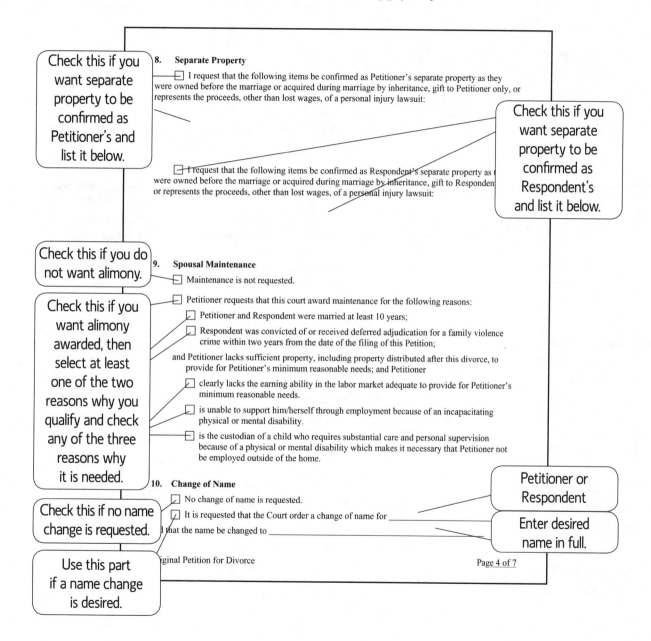

Check this if you want separate property to be confirmed as Petitioner's and list it below.

8. Separate Property

☐ I request that the following items be confirmed as Petitioner's separate property as they were owned before the marriage or acquired during marriage by inheritance, gift to Petitioner only, or represents the proceeds, other than lost wages, of a personal injury lawsuit:

Check this if you want separate property to be confirmed as Respondent's and list it below.

☐ I request that the following items be confirmed as Respondent's separate property as were owned before the marriage or acquired during marriage by inheritance, gift to Respondent or represents the proceeds, other than lost wages, of a personal injury lawsuit:

Check this if you do not want alimony.

9. Spousal Maintenance

☐ Maintenance is not requested.

☐ Petitioner requests that this court award maintenance for the following reasons:

Check this if you want alimony awarded, then select at least one of the two reasons why you qualify and check any of the three reasons why it is needed.

☐ Petitioner and Respondent were married at least 10 years;

☐ Respondent was convicted of or received deferred adjudication for a family violence crime within two years from the date of the filing of this Petition;

and Petitioner lacks sufficient property, including property distributed after this divorce, to provide for Petitioner's minimum reasonable needs; and Petitioner

☐ clearly lacks the earning ability in the labor market adequate to provide for Petitioner's minimum reasonable needs.

☐ is unable to support him/herself through employment because of an incapacitating physical or mental disability.

☐ is the custodian of a child who requires substantial care and personal supervision because of a physical or mental disability which makes it necessary that Petitioner not be employed outside of the home.

10. Change of Name

☐ No change of name is requested.

☐ It is requested that the Court order a change of name for _____

Check this if no name change is requested.

Petitioner or Respondent

and that the name be changed to _____

Enter desired name in full.

Use this part if a name change is desired.

Original Petition for Divorce   Page 4 of 7

How to fill out the Petition

Fifth page

Cross out parts that do not apply to your case

Check this box if there are no minor children.

Use this if there are children and enter requested information.

Use this if you have a handicapped child of any age and enter name of the child.

If any child owns property other than personal effects, name child and list property.

See note 4 and choose box that applies to your case.

See note 3.

If children have private health insurance, enter all information requested.

If kids have no private health insurance, indicate what they do have.

11. **Children of the Marriage**

The wife is not pregnant.

☐ No unmarried children now under eighteen years of age were born to or adopted by the parties of the marriage. We do not have any children who are 18 years or older who are disabled. We do not have children together who are in need of child or medical support.

☐ The following children now under eighteen years old were born to or adopted by the parties:

Name	Age	Sex	Birth date	Birthplace
1.				
2.				
3.				
4.				
5.				

☐ _____, a child of this marriage, requires continuous care a personal supervision because of a disability and will not be capable of self-support. The Court is requested to order that payments for the support of this child be continued after the child's eighte birthday and extended for an indefinite period.

Children's Property. No property, aside from personal effects is owned by the children ab
☐ except as listed here:

☐ The husband is NOT the biological father of these children born during the marriage:

Name	Age	Sex	Birth date	Birthplace
1.				
2.				

Information required by Texas Family Code § 152.209 (check one box)
☐ Is not required because both parents reside in Texas.
☐ Is submitted in an attached affidavit as Exhibit A.
☐ Is not provided because the health, safety, or liberty of a party or child would be jeopardized by disclosure of identifying information.

Private health care coverage (choose one below)
☐ is currently in effect for the child(ren) under policy number _____ with the _____ insurance company, and _____ is responsible for paying the premium of _____ per month. Said insurance is/is not provided through employment.

☐ There is currently no private health care coverage in effect for the child(ren) and

☐ the child(ren) is/are not receiving health care under any public health care program.

☐ the child(ren) is/are receiving health care under the following public health care program(s): _____

Original Petition for Divorce   Page 5 of 7

Note 5, Health insurance. The court needs to know whether or not private health insurance is in effect and, if it is, the name of the insurance company, the policy number, the amount of the premium and whether Petitioner or Respondent is paying it, and whether coverage is provided through employment. If no private health insurance is in effect, indicate whether the child is receiving health care under any public assistance program (name the program) and whether private health insurance is available at reasonable cost to either parent. Reasonable cost = 10% of obligor's net income.

Notes for the sixth page

Note 1, Court of Continuing Jurisdiction. The judge needs to be sure that no child is the subject of another court action or order concerning its custody. If not, check the first box. If so, check the second box and give details about the court action.

Note 2, Conservatorship. Check the first box if you want joint custody. The law presumes that it is best for the children if the parents have Joint Managing Conservatorship (JMC). The hope is to provide the children with a stable, ongoing relationship with both parents. It does *not* mean that the children spend half their time with you and half their time with the other parent. It *does* mean that you both have a voice in decisions affecting them. The rights and responsibilities of both parents are spelled out in detail in your Decree.

Check the second box if there are reasons why you think Joint Managing Conservatorship will not work for your children (chapter C), but be prepared to explain to the judge what those reasons are. Indicate who you want to have sole custody (Sole Managing Conservator), and name the other parent as Possessory Conservator.

Note 3, Long-arm Jurisdiction. Use this clause only if Respondent is not a resident of Texas. Carefully read the statements under this item and check as many as are true.

Notes for the seventh page

Note 1, Personal Information. Check the first box if you plan to provide complete personal information about all parties and children in the Decree, Exhibit 6. Also check the second box if you want that information sealed from public view to protect everyone from identity theft; it will be up to the judge whether or not to grant that request. Check only the third box if you do not want to supply personal information about yourself or children to the other side because you have good reason to believe that to do so would expose you or the children to harassment or abuse.

Note 2, Prayer. If your spouse is for sure going to sign a Waiver, omit the first line requesting the Respondent be served with a Citation.

How to fill out the Petition

Sixth page

Cross out parts that do not apply to your case

> Check this if no child is or has been the subject of a court case involving custody.

> Use this for JMC. Indicate who can establish the primary residence.

> Check this for sole custody and indicate which party gets SMC and which is PC. See note 2.

> Use item 12 if Respondent is *not* a resident of Texas, and check as many boxes as are true. See chapter A3(b).

> If any child is the subject of another court case, give full details here.

> Enter Petitioner or Respondent to show who is to pay child support.

Court of Continuing Jurisdiction (check one box)

☐ No other person has a court-ordered right to be notified about this divorce. No court ordered relationship exists between the children and any other person. No other court has continuing, exclusive jurisdiction over any child in the above list.

☐ The above named children are under the continuing, exclusive jurisdiction of the _____ Judicial District of _____ County, in the state of _____, in Cause Number _____. A final order has been entered in that case, establishing custody, child support, and visitation and Petitioner does not wish to make any changes to the prior order.

Conservatorship (Custody), Possession and Support

Upon final hearing,

☐ Petitioner and Respondent should be appointed Joint Managing Conservators of the child(ren) and _____ should have the right to establish the child(ren)'s primary residence.

☐ _____ should be appointed the Sole Managing Conservator of the child(ren) and _____ should be appointed Possessory Conservator of the child(ren).

Possession should be arranged according to the best interests of the child(ren).

☐ Petitioner ☐ Respondent should be ordered to make payments for the support of the children in the manner specified by the Court.

12. **Long-arm Jurisdiction:** Respondent is not a resident of Texas, but this court may exercise personal jurisdiction over him/her because: (check all that apply)

☐ Texas is the last state where the parties lived together as husband and wife and it has been less than two years since we separated.

☐ Respondent agrees this Court may exercise personal jurisdiction over him/her.

☐ The above child(ren) (was/were) conceived in Texas and Respondent is a parent.

☐ Respondent resided in Texas and provided prenatal expenses and/or support for the child(ren).

☐ Respondent resided with the child(ren) in Texas

☐ The child(ren) reside(s) in Texas as a result of the acts or directives or with the approval of the Respondent.

Original Petition for Divorce   Page 6 of 7

How to fill out the Petition

Seventh page

Cross out parts that do not apply to your case

Check the 1st box if you will provide personal info with the Decree. Check the 2nd box if you want that info sealed from public view. Check only the 3rd box if you do not want to furnish personal info to the other side.

If your spouse will not sign a Waiver, check this.

Indicate what documents, if any, are attached.

In Travis County, you must attach the Travis County Standing Orders.

13. Personal Information (check one box)

☑ In the Final Decree of Divorce, I will include the social security and driver's license numbers, current addresses, and phone numbers for each party and child who is subject to this suit, as required by section 105.006 of the Texas Family Code.

☑ I ask the Court to seal any attachment to the Final Decree, and any Orders to Withhold Earnings that the court might issue, that disclose the Social Security and driver's license numbers, current address, and telephone numbers of parties or children in order to protect parties and children from exposure to identity theft. Such information will be provided to parties and the court but should not be made part of files to which the public has access.

☐ I ask the Court's permission not to disclose the social security and driver's license numbers, current address, and telephone numbers in the Final Decree of Divorce because providing that information is likely to cause the child or a parent harassment, abuse, serious harm, or injury.

PRAYER

☑ Petitioner prays that citation and notice be given to Respondent as required by law.

Petitioner prays that the Court grant a divorce and decree such other relief as is requested in this petition.

Petitioner prays for such other and further relief, general and special, to which Petitioner may be entitled.

Date of your signature

Your signature

Your address and phone number

Dated: _____, 20___.

_____
Petitioner, Pro Se

Address _____

_____

Phone: _____

Attachment(s) to this Petition:
☑ Exhibit A. Information Re Minors Required Under §152.209, Texas Family Code
☐ Copy of Protective Order described in item 4 above   (if applicable)
☐ Travis County Standing Order Regarding Children, Property and Conduct of Parties
(if case filed in Travis County)

Original Petition for Divorce   Page 7 of 7

The child information form

If you listed minor children in your Petition and either of the parents lives outside Texas, you *must* also complete and attach this form unless you claim in the Petition that to do so would endanger a parent or child. It provides the court with legally required information about who the child lived with and where for the past five years.

Signed and sworn before a notary. This is a sworn statement under oath and must be signed before a Notary Public. A bank or real estate office probably has one on duty, or look in your yellow pages under "Notary."

How to fill it out

Caption: The caption is filled out just as shown for the Petition.

Items 1–6. For each child, enter the requested information. First the name and age of the child, who the child is *currently* living with and at what address, followed by similar information for the past five years, along with the current address for anyone the child lived with; if you don't know that, put "unknown." The section of information for each child is fairly self-explanatory and looks like this:

> 2. _____, age ___, who lived from _____ to ___
> the present with ☐ Petitioner ☐ Respondent ☐ Other: _____
> whose current address is _____
>
> And from _____ to _____, resided at _____
> with _____, whose current address is _____
>
> And from _____ to _____, resided at _____
> with _____, whose current address is _____
>
> And from _____ to _____, resided at _____
> with _____, whose current address is _____

Items 7–9. This is where you tell the court whether or not you have been involved in any custody proceedings involving any child in the case, or know of any such proceedings, or know of any other person who has custody or claims right to custody or visitation with any child. If you do have such information, enter it where requested on the form.

Item 10. This calls to your attention your ongoing duty to update the court if any information you have given under oath changes before you get your Final Decree.

Request that information be sealed. If you have good reason to fear for the safety of yourself or the children if their location be known, you can request that this form be sealed. Very concisely, state the facts that cause your concern.

6. Notice to Your Spouse

Proper notice to Respondent is necessary to give the court power to act in your case. Chapter A3(d) explains why this is so, and here we show you how it is done.

When you appear at the hearing, it *must* appear in the court's file that notice was properly accomplished. This can be shown by:

1. The Respondent's signed Waiver, *or*
2. The Citation, signed and returned by an officer, stating that he or she personally served papers on the Respondent.

Note: If your spouse is on active military duty, then the Waiver is the *only* way you can proceed without an attorney. If this becomes a problem, call Divorce Helpline.

Using the Waiver is the easiest way to proceed because you don't need to have the Citation issued and papers served. It helps to smooth the way at the hearing, because the judge can see that your spouse is in the picture and more or less agreeable to the divorce. Filing the Waiver is free.

If your spouse will not go before a Notary Public and sign the Waiver, then don't waste your time with it. But if there is a chance, at least give it a try. Be creative—talk nice, write a letter, or have a mutual friend take the Waiver over and explain things. If your spouse still won't sign it and is *not* on active military duty, you should have the Citation served on your spouse as explained at the end of section B below. If your spouse won't sign a Waiver *and* successfully evades service, you will need help from an attorney. Call Divorce Helpline.

Lost Spouse. If you have no idea where your spouse is, you can do the Citation only by Publication or Posting. See Chapter A3(d) and the Forms folder on the CD.

A. The Waiver

What it is

The Waiver is a sworn document, signed by your spouse before a Notary Public, which states that the Petition was received and that the case can proceed without further notice. It is, in effect, a consent to an uncontested divorce.

How to fill it out

Fill out the first page as shown in the illustration. On the second page (not shown), Respondent indicates whether or not a name change is requested; the rest is for the signatures of Respondent and a Notary. Respondent must sign it before a Notary.

Then what?

1. Check it over, then make three copies.

2. Send your spouse:
   - The original and one copy of the Waiver, *and*
   - One copy of the Petition. Your spouse *must* get a copy of the Petition.

3. *Do not* allow the Waiver to be signed before the Petition is filed. File the Petition first, then give the Waiver to your spouse. If the Waiver is dated before the Petition is filed, then it is not valid, no good, void.

4. Tell your spouse that the Waiver *must* be signed before a Notary Public. The *original*, signed and notarized, is to be returned to you as soon as possible.

5. If your spouse is also going to approve the Decree as described in chapter E, then this is the best time to do it. Prepare the Decree as shown in chapter 7, send the original and one copy along with the other papers, and make sure the original Decree is returned to you after it is signed on the last page. If you are using the Decree form straight out of this book, and if any parts of it are crossed out, then your spouse should initial each and every cross-out in the margin.

6. Take the original signed and sworn Waiver down to the District Clerk's Office and file it.

B. The Citation

What it is

The Citation is a communication from the court to the Respondent, giving notice of the Petition and ordering an answer in writing within about 20 days. Unless you plan to use a Waiver, have the clerk issue the Citation when you file your Petition. To be effective, it must be properly served on the Respondent (see below).

There are two different Citation forms, one used if your spouse lives in the same county as you, and the other for out-of-county service. The only difference is in the Return portion, which is signed off by the serving officer. An out-of-county Return *must* be signed before a Notary Public.

How to fill it out

The Citation is prepared by the clerk in most Texas counties, but in a few counties the Petitioner must prepare the document and present it with the Petition at the time of filing. Call the Clerk's office and ask who is responsible for preparing it in your county. It's easy, either way. If the clerk prepares the Citation, it will probably be mailed out, either to you or to the serving officer.

How to fill out the Waiver

First page

Cause No._____

Put in your cause number.

IN THE MATTER OF THE MARRIAGE OF: IN THE DISTRICT COURT

_____, Petitioner

Fill out the caption as shown for the Petition.

AND   ____ JUDICIAL DISTRICT

_____, Respondent   _____ COUNTY, TEXAS

AND IN THE INTEREST OF _____

_____ MINOR CHILD(REN)

WAIVER OF CITATION

This can be filled out by the Notary.

THE STATE OF TEXAS
COUNTY OF _____

Your spouse's name

On this day, _____ personally appeared before me, the
undersigned authority, who being duly sworn by me, upon oath says:

I, _____, am the Respondent in this case. My address
is _____

Your spouse's name and address

I have received a file-stamped copy of the Original Petition for Divorce which I have read and
understand.

☐ I have also been given a copy of the Travis County Standing Order Regarding Children,
Property and Conduct of Parties, which takes affect automatically, and which I have read and
understand.

I hereby enter my appearance in said cause for all purposes, waive the issuance, service and
return of Citation upon me, and agree that said cause may be taken up and considered by the Court at
any time without further notice to me. I agree that this case may be heard by a duly appointed master
or referee of this court. I waive the making of a record of testimony.

Waiver of Citation   Page 1 of 2

We have included two Citation forms in this book, one for in-county and one for out-of-county service, just in case you have need of one. Fill out the one you need, as shown in the illustrations. Check it over, then make three copies.

Then what? Service of papers on Respondent

The Citation, after it is issued by the clerk, must be forwarded to an officer for personal service on your spouse. You can choose the Sheriff or Constable to do this. We recommend the Sheriff. In many counties the court will have a list of private process servers who will cost more, but they can usually serve papers faster than public officers. If you are in a hurry, ask the clerk for their list.

If service is made in the same county, some clerks collect the fee for service with the filing fee and forward the papers for you. In other counties you have to do it yourself. In all cases where service is made in another county, you will have to forward the papers and fee yourself. It's easy; just call the Sheriff in the county where Respondent can be found, tell them where Respondent is located, and ask for the correct fee and for their address where you send the papers.

Information form

It is not required, but we strongly recommend that you send an information sheet along with the Citation, giving as much information as you have about the Respondent's whereabouts and habits, together with a complete description and, if possible, a recent and clear photograph. An "Information for Service of Process" form is provided in this book for you to use. When service is made inside the county, the serving officer has two ways to get papers served: they can be personally carried out and handed over, or mailed by registered or certified mail, delivery restricted to addressee only. Let the server know if you have an idea which way would be best

Deadline

The Citation *must* be served within 90 days of the date of issuance, or else returned unserved. If, by error, it is served after the 90 days, it will be defective and will not support a valid judgment. If your spouse is not served within the 90 days, then you will either have to have a new Citation issued and forwarded for service all over again (a new try, in other words) or you will have to get help from an attorney. Call Divorce Helpline.

Hard Cases. Do not have the Citation issued until you have a good idea where the Respondent can be found, as you don't want to waste part of your 90 days trying to locate your spouse. If you think Respondent might try to avoid service, you should certainly say this on your information sheet, together with any ideas you have as to how service

How to fill out the Citation

For service within the county

Number and county of your court

Your cause number

Your name

THE STATE OF TEXAS (Respondent Within the County)

Notice to Defendant: You have been sued. You may employ an attorney. If you or your attorney do not file a written answer with the clerk who issued this citation by 10:00 a.m. on the Monday next following the expiration of twenty days after you were served this citation and petition, a default judgment may be taken against you.

TO: _____ Defendant, Greeting:

You are hereby commanded to appear by filing a written answer to the Plaintiff's Petition at or before ten o'clock a.m. of the Monday next after the expiration of twenty days after the date of service of this citation before the ____ District Court of _____ County, Texas, at the court-house of said County in the City of _____ , Texas.

Said Plaintiff's Petition was filed in said court on the ____ day of _____ , 20___ , in this case, numbered _____ , and styled

_____ , Petitioner, and _____ , Respondent.

The nature of Petitioner's demand is fully shown by a true and correct copy of the Petition accompanying this citation and made a part hereof.

The officer executing this writ shall promptly serve the same according to requirements of law, and the mandates thereof, and make due return as the law directs. Issued and given under my hand and seal of said Court at _____ , Texas, this the ____ day of _____ , 20___.

Attest: _____

Clerk, District Court, _____ County, Texas

By _____ , Deputy.

OFFICER'S RETURN

The within citation came to hand on the ____ day of _____ , 20___ , at _____ o'clock (am)(pm), and was by me executed at _____ , within the county of _____ , at _____ o'clock (am)(pm), on the ____ day of _____ , 20___ , by delivering to the within named _____ in person, a true copy of this citation, having first endorsed thereon the date of delivery, together with the accompanying true and correct copy of the Petition.

Sheriff's Fee........................ $_____

Sheriff Account
No. _____

To certify which witness my hand officially: _____

_____

Sheriff of _____ County, Texas

By _____ , Deputy

For Clerk's Use
Taxed_____
Return recorded _____

Your spouse's name

City where your court sits

Date Petition was filed

Your spouse's name

Clerk fills out this part

The rest is filled out by officer serving papers

How to fill out the Citation

For service outside the county

Number and county of your court

Your cause number

Your name

Clerk fills out this part

The rest is filled out by officer serving papers

Your spouse's name

City where your court sits

Date Petition was filed

Your spouse's name

THE STATE OF TEXAS   (Respondent Without the County)

   Notice to Defendant: You have been sued. You may employ an attorney. If you or your attorney do not file a written answer with the clerk who issued this citation by 10:00 a.m. on the Monday next following the expiration of twenty days after you were served this citation and petition, a default judgment may be taken against you.

TO: _____ Defendant, Greeting:

   You are hereby commanded to appear by filing a written answer to the Plaintiff's Petition at or before ten o'clock a.m. of the Monday next after the expiration of twenty days after the date of service of this citation before the ____ District Court of _____ County, Texas, at the courthouse of said County in the City of _____ ,Texas.

   Said Plaintiff's Petition was filed in said court on the ____ day of _____, 20___, in this case, numbered _____, and styled

_____, Petitioner, and _____, Respondent.

   The nature of Petitioner's demand is fully shown by a true and correct copy of the Petition accompanying this citation and made a part hereof.

   The officer executing this writ shall promptly serve the same according to requirements of law, and the mandates thereof, and make due return as the law directs. Issued and given under my hand and seal of said Court at _____, Texas, this the ____ day of _____, 20___.
      Attest: _____
      Clerk, District Court, _____ County, Texas
      By _____ , Deputy.

                              RETURN

The State of _____
County of _____
   Before me, the undersigned authority, on this day personally appeared _____ _____,a person not interested in the within-mentioned suit, above 21 years of age, of sound mind and competent to make oath, and being sworn, deposed and said:
   My name is _____; I am disinterested in the within styled and numbered cause, above 21 years of age, of sound mind and competent to make oath of the facts below:
   The within citation came to hand on the ____ day of _____, 20___ at _____ o'clock (am)(pm), and was by me executed at _____, within the county of _____ at _____ o'clock (am)(pm), on the ____ day of _____, 20___, by delivering to the within named _____ in person, a true copy of this citation, having first endorsed thereon the date of delivery, together with the accompanying true and correct copy of the Petition.
   The distance actualy travelled by me in serving such process was _____ miles, and my fees are as follows: For serving this citation .... $ _____
                           For mileage .... $ _____
                           For notary .... $ _____
                                    Total fees .... $ _____

| **Sheriff Account** |
| No. _____ |

   To certify which witness my hand officially: _____
   Signed and sworn to by the said _____ before me this _____ day of _____, 20___ to certify which witness my hand and seal of office.

| **For Clerk's Use** |
| Taxed _____ |
| Return recorded _____ . |

_____
Notary Public, _____ County,
_____. (or other competent officer.)

can best be accomplished. If, during the 90 days, you get better information as to how the Respondent can be found and served, don't delay getting this information to the serving officer. If it is near the end of the 90-day period when you get a hot lead, then it is best to have a new Citation issued.

The serving officer is unlikely to do anything creative about finding and serving your spouse. It is *your* responsibility to give the best and most complete information you can about how to locate and identify your spouse. Dig hard. Talk to people; write, call, be a detective. Make your information sheet very complete, clear, and specific.

Citation and Service of Process checklist

1. File the Petition

- Take in your information sheet.
- Take in the Citation, too, in those counties where the clerk does not make it up for you.
- Tell the clerk that you want the Sheriff to serve the papers.

2. Forward the papers to the Sheriff

Forward them to the Sheriff of the county where the Respondent is to be served. Where service is to be in your own county, the clerk may do this, but in cases where you do it and not the clerk, then:

- Call the Sheriff's office and ask how much the service will cost.
- Send the original Citation, the information sheet, and a copy of the Petition, include a money order for the fees charged by the Sheriff.
- Tell the out-of-county Sheriff that the return must be sworn before a Notary Public according to Texas law.

3. Return of Citation

- It will be returned blank if service was not made. It will be filled out and signed if service was successful.
- If forwarded to the Sheriff by the clerk, it will be returned to the clerk, with notice by post card to you. You should go down to the Clerk's office to make sure it is really on file, accurately filled out, and signed by the officer.
- If forwarded by you, it will come back to you. You should check the return over and quickly get it on file at the District Clerk's office.
- If service was not made, contact the Sheriff to find out what the problem was. You can either send out a new Citation and try one more time, or you can refer the case to an attorney for help. Call Divorce Helpline.

7. The Decree

What it is

After listening to your testimony at the hearing, the judge will verbally make findings and issue orders; that's your judgment. The clerk will take notes on the docket sheet as evidence of the decision. You must prepare a Decree, a typed statement of the judgment, that will be signed by the judge and filed. In most cases, your Decree will include some attachments (Exhibits) that are part of the Decree.

How to fill it out

Since you usually get what you request in uncontested cases, prepare the Decree and any necessary Exhibits before the hearing and take them with you so the Decree can be signed then and there. If the judge decides differently from your Decree, go home and do a different Decree to match the judge's order and send it in (through the clerk) for signing. Fill out the Decree and needed attachments as described below. See chapter 3A about how to use the paper forms or edit the computer files on the CD. If you are using the paper forms from the back of this book, and if the Decree is being approved by your spouse on the last page, your spouse should also initial crossed-out parts.

Exhibits

In cases with children, or property or debts to be divided, the Decree uses attachments, called Exhibits, to provide orders on those subjects. Use any that are relevant to your case. Exhibits are listed alphabetically, in the order they are mentioned in the Decree, so the first one you mention will be Exhibit A, the next will be Exhibit B, and so on. There are seven possible Exhibits:

Children's Property	Used if a child owns property
Conservatorship Order	Used in any case with a minor child
Standard Possession Order	Used in any case with a minor child
Child Support Order	Used in any case with a minor child
Health Insurance Order	Used in any case with a minor child
Required Information	Used in every case
Orders Re Property and Debts	Used if you divide property or debts

Then what?

If you are going to have an approved Decree (chapter E), have your spouse initial any crossed-out parts and sign the last page as described in chapter E, section 1, *then* make copies with your spouse's signature on it. In addition to any Exhibits that go with the

How to fill out the Decree

First page

Cause No._____

IN THE MATTER OF THE MARRIAGE OF: IN THE DISTRICT COURT

_____, Petitioner

_____ JUDICIAL DISTRICT

AND

_____, Respondent   _____ COUNTY, TEXAS

AND IN THE INTEREST OF _____

_____ MINOR CHILD(REN)

FINAL DECREE OF DIVORCE

On the ___ day of _____, 20___, final hearing was held in this cause.

Petitioner, _____, who is the ☐ husband, ☐ wife, appeared in person, pro se, and announced ready for trial.

Respondent, _____

☐ personally appeared.
☐ has agreed to the terms of this Decree.
☐ was duly and properly cited by personal service and failed to appear.
☐ waived issuance and service of citation by Waiver of Citation duly filed.

☐ A record of testimony was made.
☐ The making of a record of testimony was waived by the parties with consent of the Court.

Because a jury was not demanded by either party, the Court tried the cause.

The Court, after reviewing the pleadings and receiving evidence, finds that the pleadings are in due form; that all residence requirements and prerequisites of law have been legally satisfied; that this Court has personal jurisdiction of the parties and of the subject matter of this cause; and that the material allegations of the Petition are true.

1.   **Divorce**

THE COURT FINDS that Petitioner and Respondent were married, and that their marriage had become insupportable and without any reasonable expectation of reconciliation.

THE COURT ORDERS that the marriage of Petitioner and Respondent is dissolved and that they are hereby divorced.

Final Decree of Divorce   Page 1 of 6

Callout labels:

- Date of hearing
- Fill out caption as shown on page 81.
- Your name
- Spouse's name
- Use this if your spouse was served with papers.
- Use this if your spouse signed a Waiver.
- Indicate if a court reporter did or did not make a record.

Decree, if you have a settlement agreement, attach a copy to each copy of the Decree. If you use the Withholding Order (chapter 9), attach a copy to each copy of the Decree. Be sure to keep all originals together. Do not attach the Request to Issue Withholding Order to the Decree—it goes separately to the clerk.

Check over the forms for accuracy, make four copies of each, and take all originals and copies with you to the hearing.

Notes for the second page

Item 2. If you have no minor children, state that fact and move on to page 4, item 8. Cross out or delete all other items about children. If you do have children, enter identifying information about each child.

At the end of the list of minor children, the court makes a finding that no child has significant property other than personal belongings. If this is not true, check the box and attach an Exhibit that names the child and lists the child's property. Use Ex1 on the CD, or simply take a plain sheet of paper and at the top center put the title, "Exhibit A: Property Belonging to Children," and under that heading make a list.

Next comes a place for you to list any children born during the marriage who are not the biological children of the husband. If none, cross out or delete this part.

Item 3. If you have minor children, you *must* complete and attach the Conservatorship Orders as an Exhibit.

Exhibit: Conservatorship Orders

This is where you define the rights and duties of each parent. At the top of page 1, enter your cause number and the Exhibit number. Then indicate how you want custody to be ordered, like this:

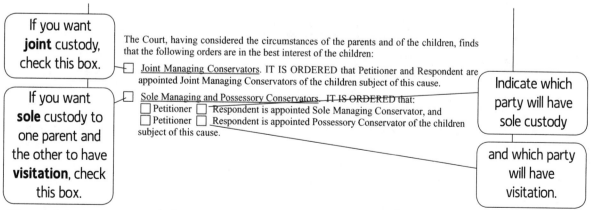

Texas law presumes joint custody is best for the children, so if you request sole custody, be prepared to explain why this is better when you get to court.

How to fill out the Decree

Second page

Cross out parts that do not apply to your case

> **Check this box if there are no minor children. See notes.**

> **Check this box if there are minor children. See notes.**

> **Check this box if any minor owns property and attach Ex1 (on the CD) as Exhibit A.**

> **If there are minor children, attach Conservatorship Orders for their custody.**

> **Give information requested for each child. See notes.**

> **Check this box if the husband is not the biological father of any child born during marriage.**

2. **Children of the Marriage**

☐ THE COURT FINDS that there is no unmarried child of the marriage under eighteen years of age and none is expected and that there are no children of the marriage over 18 who are disabled.

☐ THE COURT FINDS that Petitioner and Respondent are the parents of the following children:

Name:_____ Sex:___ Age:____ Birth date: _____
Present residence: _____
Birthplace: _____ Home State: _____

Name:_____ Sex:___ Age:____ Birth date: _____
Present residence: _____
Birthplace: _____ Home State: _____

Name:_____ Sex:___ Age:____ Birth date: _____
Present residence: _____
Birthplace: _____ Home State: _____

Name:_____ Sex:___ Age:____ Birth date: _____
Present residence: _____
Birthplace: _____ Home State: _____

Name:_____ Sex:___ Age:____ Birth date: _____
Present residence: _____
Birthplace: _____ Home State: _____

THE COURT FINDS that there are no other children of the marriage under age 18 or other entitled to support and that none are expected.

THE COURT FINDS that the children do not own or possess any property other than personal effects ☐ except as stated in Exhibit ___.

☐ The husband is **NOT** the biological father of the following children born during the marriage and that no legal relationship exists between these children and the husband:

Name:_____ Sex:___ Age:____ Birth date: _____

Name:_____ Sex:___ Age:____ Birth date: _____

Name:_____ Sex:___ Age:____ Birth date: _____

3. **Conservatorship** (custody)

THE COURT ORDERS that conservatorship, rights, duties, and responsibilities are awarded as provided in Exhibit ___, which is attached and incorporated into this Decree for all purposes.

Final Decree of Divorce   Page 2 of 6

Sections A and B spell out parents' rights in detail, so be sure to read it very carefully and, if possible, discuss it with the other parent. There are no choices to make.

Page 2, Section C. You must choose who has the right to decide the child's primary residence and whether the choice is limited to any particular geographical area.

Page 3, Section D. You must check boxes to show how the parents will share various rights and duties. Read this section carefully and for *each* item, indicate whether those matters will be under the authority of one parent, the other parent, both together, or each to have authority without consulting the other.

Notes for the third page

Item 4. Enter the Exhibit number for your Possession Order, the schedule by which the parents will share the care of their child(ren). Next, check a box to choose (again) which parent will be the Home Parent, making sure it is the same on all documents.

Children under three. If you want a different schedule for children under three, check this box and attach a second schedule for babies who will then come under the first schedule on their third birthdays.

Item 5. Enter the Exhibit number for the child support order.

Item 6. Enter the Exhibit number for the health insurance order.

Item 7. Warnings and notices. Read very carefully. Do not edit or alter.

Exhibit: Possession Order

The exhibit provided in this book is the Standard Possession Order (SPO). Read chapter C section 3 and study this Exhibit (back of book) very carefully. Notice the places with blanks or check boxes where you must indicate times or make choices.

Whatever your custody order says, it is your Possession Order that determines when each parent will have the child. Parents are free to care for the child however they like by agreement, but when they don't agree, they must abide by their Possession Order. The SPO will be issued in any case where parents can't agree on their own schedule. Parents can agree to almost any reasonable schedule so long there is a similar degree of detail as in the SPO. If there's no agreement in an MSA or approved Decree signed by your spouse, and if you wander far from the SPO, a judge may ask you to explain. If you want restricted visitation or no visitation at all, consult an attorney, call Divorce Helpline, or contact one of the Attorney General's Visitation Centers for help.

Note. If you modify the SPO (back of book and on CD) more than a little, remove the word "Standard" from the title and just call it a Possession Order, so the judge will know it is not the same as the Standard Possession Order.

If you want a separate schedule for a child under three, prepare two schedules. The first one is the "Possession Order," with the schedule for children over three, and the second is the "Possession Order for Children Under Three," which you make by altering the first one to suit the needs of the infant.

Exhibit: Child Support Order

Page 1. At the top, enter the cause and Exhibit numbers, then indicate which party pays (obligor) and which party receives (obligee) child support payments.

Next, choose whether to use Section A or B for your support order.

> • **Section A.** Use this section if there is only one child or if parents have agreed that the amount of support will remain the same until the last child is no longer eligible to receive support. Enter the total amount to be paid, adding to guideline support any additional amount ordered to cover health insurance (chapter D5).

> • **Section B** (page 2). Used if there is more than one child, it orders a specific lower amount each time a child becomes ineligible to receive support. Fill in the beginning total amount, then the new amount to be paid each time a child becomes ineligible, for as many times as there are children to support. Unless you agree otherwise in writing, each amount should at least equal guideline for the remaining children plus additional support amounts ordered to cover their health insurance (chapter D5).

Page 3, Section C. This section *must* be used and completely filled out whenever your order is significantly above or below the Texas child support guidelines (chapter D). Net resource figures are described in chapter D2. Item 5 is asking about obligor's (payor's) minor children of other relationships who live with obligor and who obligor has a duty to support. Item 8 (page 4) requests a narrative explanation for why the amount to be ordered is different from the guideline.

Page 4, Section E. Use this section if you do not want the paying spouse's wages to be attached so long as he/she stays current with support payments.

Page 5, Section H. Check with your court clerk to verify the address where they want child support payments sent. Counties might vary on this.

Page 5, Section I. Use this section in any county with a Domestic Relations Office where they want you to open an account for child support payments. Ask the clerk.

Exhibit: Health Insurance Order

See Chapter D5. The amount paid for health insurance should be added to the amount for guideline child support to produce the total support ordered in the Support Order.

Page 1. Enter the cause number and the Exhibit number. At item 1, indicate who pays for the health insurance and, at item 2, indicate who will receive it.

Page 2, item 8. Use this section if the recipient pays for child support and is reimbursed by the payor in payor's monthly child support payments.

Page 2, item 10. Use this section if health insurance is not affordable by either parent.

Notes for the fourth page

First line. If the judge agreed that you have shown a good reason to believe that furnishing the identifying information could expose the party or a child to harassment or abuse, check a box to show which party is excused.

Item 8, Required Information.

1.   Unless the judge agreed that you are excused, you have to check the first box, enter the number of the Required Information Exhibit, and attach it to the Decree.

2.   Sealing personal information from public view is good common sense, but not required by law. It might be best to leave this paragraph in your Decree with the boxes blank, and at the hearing remember to ask the judge to protect your family from identity theft by ordering the information sealed from public view.

3.   If you were able to give the judge a good reason why furnishing identifying information would expose a party or child to harassment or abuse, check the third box and do not attach the Required Information exhibit. You might bring it to court in case the judge doesn't think your evidence of threat is convincing. If that happens, refer the judge to item 2 above and ask to have the information sealed.

> **8.   Information Regarding Parties And Children**
> **Required by Section 105.006 of the Texas Family Code**
>
> ☐ The information required by § 105.006 of the Texas Family Code is attached in Exhibit ___, which is incorporated herein for all purposes.
>
> ☐ **Protection from identity theft.** The information required by § 105.006 of the Texas Family Code is attached in Exhibit ___, which is incorporated herein for all purposes. THE COURT FINDS that making personal information available to the public would expose the parties ☐ and their child(ren) to unnecessary risk of identity theft. THEREFORE IT IS ORDERED that ☐ this Exhibit ☐ the Decree and all attachments be sealed and made unavailable to the public.
>
> ☐ **Protection from abuse.** THE COURT FINDS, pursuant to Texas Family Code section 105.006(c), requiring ☐ Petitioner ☐ Respondent to provide the information required by section 105.006 is likely to cause the party or a child harassment, abuse, serious harm or injury. Accordingly, IT IS ORDERED that ☐ Petitioner ☐ Respondent is not required to provide the information required by Texas Family Code section 105.006.

Exhibit: Required Information

Enter cause number and Exhibit number at the top. Enter requested information for each party and child (if any). Try to get it all, as it will help if enforcement is required.

If you don't know an item, put "unknown." If a child has no Social Security number, contact the Social Security office to get one, as it is necessary for the enforcement of support orders. Enter driver's license numbers for children who have them, otherwise type in "none."

Notes for the fifth page

Fill it out as shown in the illustration. If you have any separate property to be confirmed to one spouse or the other, or any community property or debts to be divided, you will want to use the Exhibit, Orders Re Property and Debts.

Item 9, Property and Debts. If you listed separate or community property on your Petition and it was not later divided by written agreement, then it will be confirmed and/or divided by the judge, probably just as you request (if your request is reasonable). Use the third option, enter the Exhibit number, and attach the Orders Re Property and Debts exhibit to show what separate property (if any) is being confirmed to one party or the other, and what community property is awarded to Petitioner, what property to Respondent, which debts are assigned to Petitioner, and which debts are assigned to Respondent.

Item 10, Income Taxes. Use the second clause to assign rights and responsibilities to the spouses for income tax liability or refunds due for periods prior to the divorce. The percentages used can be whatever you agree to—for example, a ratio of the incomes of the spouses—or all could be assigned to one spouse or the other as part of the overall property division.

Item 11, Spousal Maintenance. Use this section if there will be an award of spousal maintenance. Fill it out as shown in the illustration. The actual support order appears at the top of the sixth page of the Decree.

Exhibit: Orders Re Property and Debts

Top. Enter your cause number and the Exhibit number.

How to list property and debts. When you list property or debts, number each item in each list. Use the same description as in the Petition, but you need not put down the value of items. Give license and vehicle ID numbers for any vehicles that are awarded.

Real Estate. If real property is confirmed or awarded, you should use language like this when you list it:

> (Item number) "The following real property, including escrow funds, prepaid insurance, utility deposits, keys, and title documents: . . . " (give the address(es) as well as full legal description(s), as shown in chapter 5, third page of the Petition)."

How to fill out the Decree

Fifth page

Cross out parts that do not apply to your case

Check this box if there is no separate or community property.

Check this box if you are attaching a settlement agreement.

Check this box if you have property or debts to divide and enter the number of the Property and Debts exhibit.

9. Separate and Community Property and Debts

☐ THE COURT FINDS THAT the parties do not own any separate or community property of any significant value other than their personal effects. IT IS ORDERED that each party is awarded the personal effects presently in his/her possession as his/her separate property.

☐ THE COURT FINDS THAT the parties have entered into a written agreement for the division of their property and debts and that the agreement is just and right. IT IS ORDERED that the agreement of the parties, which is attached hereto and incorporated herein for all purposes, be and is approved.

☐ THE COURT FINDS THAT the parties possess separate and/or community property and debts which should be justly confirmed and/or divided. IT IS ORDERED that the estate of the parties is divided as set forth in Exhibit ___, which is attached and incorporated into this Decree for all purposes.

10. Income Taxes

THE COURT ORDERS that Petitioner and Respondent shall each be responsible for all taxes attributable to their own income only and each entitled to their own refunds for the year of the divorce.

☐ IT IS FURTHER ORDERED that Petitioner shall pay ___ percent and Respondent shall pay ___ percent of any income tax liability accrued prior to the year of the divorce, and that Petitioner shall receive ___ percent and Respondent shall receive ___ percent of any income tax refund accrued prior to the year of the divorce.

Use these clauses if you want orders about who pays or receives income taxes from before the divorce.

11. Spousal Maintenance

☐ The Court finds maintenance should be awarded on the following grounds:

☐ Petitioner and Respondent were married at least ten (10) years.

☐ Respondent was convicted of or received deferred adjudication for a family violence crime within two years from the date of the filing of this Petition.

In addition to the above, Petitioner lacks sufficient property, including property distributed after this divorce, to provide for Petitioner's minimum reasonable needs; and Petitioner

☐ clearly lacks the earning ability in the labor market adequate to provide for Petitioner's minimum reasonable needs.

☐ is unable to support him/herself through employment because of an incapacitating physical or mental disability.

☐ is the custodian of a child of this marriage who requires substantial care and personal supervision because of a physical or mental disability which makes it necessary that Petitioner not be employed outside of the home.

If alimony is to be ordered, check one or both boxes to indicate grounds.

And also check boxes to show one or more reasons that justify spousal maintenance.

Final Decree of Divorce

Page 5 of 6

Stock and the like. Enter brokerage name, account number, stock or fund symbol, and number of shares.

Groupings. It is okay to make general groupings of items, similar to those on the property checklist in chapter B3. For example, "All household goods and appliances currently in the possession of (party), subject to his/her sole control, except as otherwise expressly awarded to (other party)." You should list separately any items of significant value or personal meaning.

Section A, Separate Property. Use section A1 to list separate property or debts being confirmed to Petitioner and section A2 for Respondent.

Section B is used to divide community property.

Section B1, Employee Retirement Plans. It is much cleaner and simpler if you can arrange to award all of a defined benefit pension plan to the employee-spouse. If you can't arrange this, use this section. The court retains jurisdiction over the plan, and the employee is ordered not to apply for or accept benefits under the plan without notifying the other spouse, but **(warning!)** you *must* seek to clarify or divide rights in the plan within two years or lose the right. Better talk to an attorney if this is what you plan to do. Call Divorce Helpline.

Section B2 is where you award Petitioner's share of the community property. Use any of the subsections that apply to your case.

Section B3 is the allocation of Petitioner's share of the community debts. Use any of the subsections that apply to your case. Be careful to list here any debts associated with property being kept by Petitioner unless you intentionally agreed to share the obligation after your divorce.

Section B4 is where you award Respondent's share of the community property. Use any of the subsections that apply to your case.

Section B5 is the allocation of Respondent's share of the community debts. Use any of the subsections that apply to your case. Be careful to list here any debts associated with property being kept by Respondent unless you intentionally agreed to share the obligation after your divorce.

About the sixth page

Fill it out as shown in the illustration. If your Possession Order varies more than a little from the Standard Possession Order form in the back of the book and on our CD, remove the word "Standard" from the Exhibit title here and on the Possession Order itself. This is so the judge will know it is not the standard order.

How to fill out the Decree

Sixth page

Cross out parts that do not apply to your case

> **Indicate who pays whom, when payments begin, how much per month, and how many months it continues.**

THEREFORE, THE COURT ORDERS that ☐ Petitioner ☐ Respondent pay to ☐ Petitioner ☐ Respondent for spousal maintenance the sum of $_____ per month, due and payable beginning _____, 20___ and continuing on the same day of each month thereafter until either party dies; or the receiving party remarries. This order for maintenance shall continue for ____ months or further order of this court. All payments shall be made to any address designated in writing by the recipient.

12. Mediation

THE COURT ORDERS, and the Parties agree, that in the event disputes arise between the parties, the parties will seek mediation to resolve the disputes before any judicial proceeding, unless the matter to be determined concerns a serious question regarding the health and safety of the child.

> **Use this part if there is to be a name change.**

13. Name Change

☐ IT IS ORDERED AND DECREED THAT the name of _____ is hereby changed back to _____.

> **Petitioner or Respondent**

> **Put in desired name, in full.**

Signed and entered this ____ day of _____, 20___.

_____
Judge Presiding

Exhibits Attached:

> **List and number all Exhibits that are attached.**

☐ Exhibit __ Property Owned by Children
☐ Exhibit __ Conservatorship
☐ Exhibit __ Standard Possession Order
☐ Exhibit __ Possession Order for Children Under Three Years
☐ Exhibit __ Child Support Order
☐ Exhibit __ Health Insurance for Children
☐ Exhibit __ Information Required by Texas Family Code § 105.006
☐ Exhibit __ Orders re Property and Debts

I approve and consent as to both form and substance:

Date: _____   Date: _____

_____   _____
Petitioner   Respondent

> **If Decree is approved by your spouse, both spouses sign here. See chapter E section 1.**

...e of Divorce   Page 6 of 6

8. The Statistics Form

Information on Suit
Affecting the Family Relationship

What is it?

Although the court already has a file full of information about your divorce, they need this additional form to track and report the basics of your case to the Bureau of Vital Statistics. When there are children, the State Case Registry uses it for tracking support orders and payments. The Bureau of Vital Statistics uses the basic information about your divorce for their periodic statistical reports.

How to fill it out

Fill it out as shown on the next three pages.

Then what?

Make one copy of the completed form for your own files and take the original with you to the hearing. The clerk will ask for it at the right time.

Note! This form *must* be printed on two sides of one page, not two separate pages.

Notes for the front side

There is no need to cross out unused sections on this form.

Section 1. The information for item 1 comes from the caption on your divorce forms. At item 3, check one of the top boxes to indicate whether or not your divorce involves children. At item 4, because you are representing yourself, enter your own name, phone, and address. Your name should be followed by a comma and the words Pro Se. Leave box 4b blank.

Section 2. Fill in all requested information. If no children, enter "0" at item 17.

Section 3. Fill in as many segments as you have children. If more than four children, attach an additional form marked "continuation" at the top and attach it to the original form. As children of divorce do not typically get new names, nor are they typically known by a prior name (a.k.a.), most people will leave items f and g blank.

Notes for the back side

Section 4. Must be completed if there is child support. "Obligee" is the parent receiving support and "obligor #1" is the parent who pays support. Check box 25c or 25d to show if obligee is the husband or wife, then complete only items 31 and 32. Next, check box 33b or 33c to show if obligor #1 is the husband or the wife, then complete only items 39 to 43.

Section 5. Leave blank.

Section 6. Leave blank.

Information on Suit
Affecting the Family Relationship

Front side

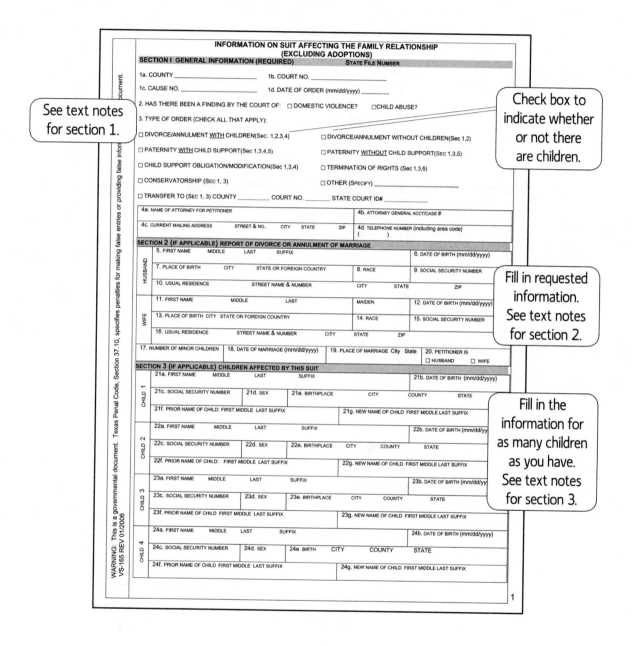

Information on Suit
Affecting the Family Relationship

Back side

See text notes for filling out section 4.

Leave this part blank.

Leave the rest blank.

SECTION 4 (IF APPLICABLE) OBLIGEE/OBLIGOR INFORMATION

THIS PARTY TO THE SUIT IS (CHECK ONE)   ☐25a. TDPRS   ☐ 25b. NON-PARENT CONSERVATOR – COMPLETE 26 – 32

☐ 25c. HUSBAND AS SHOWN ON FRONT OF THIS FORM – COMPLETE 31 – 32 ONLY   ☐ 25d. WIFE AS SHOWN ON FRONT OF THIS FORM – COMPLETE 31 – 32 ONLY

☐ 25e. BIOLOGICAL FATHER – COMPLETE 26 – 32   ☐ 25f. BIOLOGICAL MOTHER – COMPLETE 26 – 32

26. FIRST NAME	MIDDLE	LAST	SUFFIX	MAIDEN

27. DATE OF BIRTH (mm/dd/yyyy)	28. PLACE OF BIRTH	CITY	STATE OR FOREIGN COUNTRY

29. USUAL RESIDENCE	STREET NAME & NUMBER	CITY	COUNTY	STATE	ZIP

30. SOCIAL SECURITY NUMBER	31. DRIVER LICENSE NO & STATE	32. TELEPHONE NUMBER ( )

THIS PARTY TO THE SUIT IS (CHECK ONE)   ☐ 33a. NON-PARENT CONSERVATOR – COMPLETE 34 – 43

☐ 33b. HUSBAND AS SHOWN ON FRONT OF THIS FORM – COMPLETE 39 – 43 ONLY   ☐33c. WIFE AS SHOWN ON FRONT OF THIS FORM – COMPLETE 39 – 43 ONLY

☐33d. BIOLOGICAL FATHER – COMPLETE 34 – 43   ☐ 33e. BIOLOGICAL MOTHER – COMPLETE 34 – 43

OBLIGOR #1

34. FIRST NAME	MIDDLE	LAST	SUFFIX	MAIDEN

35. DATE OF BIRTH (mm/dd/yyyy)	36. PLACE OF BIRTH	CITY	STATE OR FOREIGN COUNTRY

37. USUAL RESIDENCE	STREET NAME & NUMBER	CITY	COUNTY	STATE	ZIP

38. SOCIAL SECURITY NUMBER	39 DRIVER LICENSE NO. & STATE	40. TELEPHONE NUMBER ( )

41. EMPLOYER NAME	42. EMPLOYER TELEPHONE NUMBER

43. EMPLOYER PAYROLL ADDRESS	STREET NAME & NUMBER	CITY	STATE	ZIP

THIS PARTY TO THE SUIT IS (CHECK ONE)   ☐ 44a. NON-PARENT CONSERVATOR – COMPLETE 45 – 54

☐ 44b. HUSBAND AS SHOWN ON FRONT OF THIS FORM – COMPLETE 50 – 54 ONLY   ☐ 44c. WIFE AS SHOWN ON FRONT OF THIS FORM – COMPLETE 45 – 54 ONLY

☐ 44d. BIOLOGICAL FATHER – COMPLETE 45 – 54   ☐ 44e. BIOLOGICAL MOTHER – COMPLETE 45 – 54

45. FIRST NAME	MIDDLE	LAST	SUFFIX	MAIDEN

46. DATE OF BIRTH (mm/dd/yyyy)	47. PLACE OF BIRTH	CITY	STATE OR FOREIGN COUNTRY

48. USUAL RESIDENCE	STREET NAME & NUMBER	CITY	COUNTY	STATE	ZIP

49. SOCIAL SECURITY NUMBER	50. DRIVER LICENSE NO & STATE	51. TELEPHONE NUMBER

52. EMPLOYER NAME	53. EMPLOYER TELEPHONE NUMBER

54. EMPLOYER PAYROLL ADDRESS	STREET NAME & NUMBER	CITY	STATE	ZIP

SECTION 5 (IF APPLICABLE) FOR ORDERS CONCERNING PATERNITY ESTABLISHMENT OF BIOLOGICAL FATHER

55. BIOLOGICAL FATHER'S NAME	FIRST	MIDDLE	LAST	56. DATE OF BIRTH (mm/dd/yyyy)

57. SOCIAL SECURITY NUMBER	58. CURRENT MAILING ADDRESS	STREET NAME & NUMBER	CITY	STATE	ZIP

DOES THIS ORDER REMOVE INFORMATION PERTAINING TO A FATHER FROM A CHILD'S CERTIFICATE OF BIRTH? ☐ NO   ☐ YES

SECTION 6 TERMINATION OF RIGHTS – INFORMATION RELATED TO THE INDIVIDUAL(S) WHOSE RIGHTS ARE BEING TERMINATED IN THIS SUIT.

FIRST NAME	MIDDLE NAME	LAST NAME	SUFFIX	60b. RELATIONSHIP
61a. FIRST NAME	MIDDLE NAME	LAST NAME	SUUFIX	61b. RELATIONSHIP
62a. FIRST NAME	MIDDLE NAME	LAST NAME	SUFFIX	62b. RELATIONSHIP

COMMENTS: _____

_____

I CERTIFY THAT THE ABOVE ORDER WAS GRANTED ON THE
DATE AND PLACE AS STATED.

_____
SIGNATURE OF THE CLERK OF THE COURT

9. The Withholding Forms

What they are

Use these forms if child support or spousal maintenance will be ordered.

A. Which withholding order to use

1. Child support. If child support will be ordered, you *must* fill out the Employer's Order to Withhold Income for Child Support and take it to the hearing with your Decree.

2. Spousal maintenance. Income withholding for spousal maintenance can be ordered if payments are imposed by a court, but *not* for spousal maintenance agreed by the parties unless your contract specifically permits it. If you will have an order for spousal maintenance imposed by the court, you must fill out and file the Employer's Order to Withhold Earnings for Spousal Maintenance and take it to the hearing with your Decree.

No exceptions. Even if the obligee is self-employed, unemployed, or can't be found, you must nonetheless file the withholding order. The order will remain on file until the obligor has wages that support can be withheld from or until the entire support obligation, including arrearages, is completely paid.

B. The Request to Issue Order to Withhold Earnings

When you are ready to have the Clerk's Office send your withholding order to the obligor's employer, use this Request to Issue form. File it with the District Clerk and pay a nominal filing fee, about $20. If the obligor changes jobs, you can file a new Request to Issue form naming the new employer.

Page 2 of the Order to Withhold Income for Child Support tells the employer that a copy of Subchapter C, Chapter 158, of the Family Code is attached to this form. If the clerk does not provide this (you can ask them), you will find it on the CD that comes with this book in the Forms Etc folder, form 07A. It is only four pages long.

Cooperation. If you and your Ex are on good terms, you can agree that you will not request the clerk to issue the withholding orders so long as support payments are not more than a certain number of days late. Best to do this in writing, at least a signed letter, so you can later remind one another what you agreed to. However, if the supported children are receiving public assistance, this form *must* be issued, no exceptions.

C. How to fill out the Employer's Order to Withhold Income for Child Support

Note 1. Fill out the caption just like the other forms. Use the full names of children.

Note 2. Pages 1 and 2. Enter requested information for each child. If the child does not yet have a Social Security number, enter "none." It would be best to apply for one now.

Note 3. Page 2, Method of Payment, item 2. Enter your case number.

Note 4. Page 3, Order to Withhold. Enter the amount to be withheld in the section that corresponds to obligor's pay period, following instructions that appear on the form.

Note 5. Page 4. If you have more than one child, you need to enter the amounts of support that will be due after each child becomes ineligible to receive support for any of the reasons listed on page 3. You can agree on these amounts ahead of time with obligor or you can simply follow guideline support for the reduced number of children. Don't forget, if circumstances change as time goes by, either of you can apply for a modification of the child support order.

Note 6. Page 5. At the bottom, check the box if the court issued a Medical Child Support Order, ordering the employer to provide health insurance coverage for the children.

Employer's Order to Withhold Income for Child Support

Page 1

CAUSE NO. _____

IN THE MATTER OF THE MARRIAGE OF

_____ §

Petitioner [Print your full name]

AND §

_____ §

Respondent [Print your spouse's full name] §

AND IN THE INTEREST OF §

MINOR CHILDREN: §

_____ §

_____ §

_____ §

_____ §

_____ §

_____ §

[Print the full names of your children]

IN THE DISTRICT COURT OF

COUNTY, TEXAS

#_____ JUDICIAL DISTRICT

> Fill out caption as shown on page 81.

> Use full names for children.

EMPLOYER'S ORDER TO WITHHOLD FROM EARNINGS FOR CHILD SUPPORT

The Court ORDERS you, the employer of _____, Obligor, to withhold income from the Obligor's disposable earnings from this employment as follows:

> Name of person paying child support, called the "obligor"

OBLIGOR: *(the person who pays child support)*

Name: _____ Social security Number _____

Address: _____

OBLIGEE: *(the person who receives child support)*

Name: _____ Social security Number _____

Address: _____

CHILDREN:

1. **Child's name** _____

Date of Birth: _____ Social Security #: _____

Date child turns 18 _____ Place of Birth: _____

> Information about the person who will be paying support

> Information about the person who will be receiving support, called the "obligee"

> Information about each child

Withholding Order   Page 1 of 5

D. How to fill out the Employer's Order to Withhold Earnings for Spousal Maintenance

Note 1. Fill out the caption just like all the other forms.

Note 2. Fill in the requested information for the obligor (the person ordered to pay spousal maintenance) and the obligee (the person receiving spousal maintenance).

Note 3, Privacy. In cases where you need to protect the location of a party, you can omit your place of residence, but you might have to explain your reasons at a hearing.

Notes for the second page

Under "Order to Withhold," fill in all four blanks in this section. At line (1), enter the full monthly amount of spousal maintenance. For line (2), multiply the full monthly amount by .50 and enter the result here. For line (3), multiply by .4615, and for line (4), multiply by .2308.

In the next blank, enter the date the court ordered the spousal maintenance to terminate. If the court ordered maintenance for 24 months, enter the last day of the 24th month from the date the court signs this order.

Then what?

Make four copies and take them to court with your Decree. Be sure to keep the originals together. You will take these with you to the hearing.

Employer's Order to Withhold Earnings for Spousal Maintenance

First page

CAUSE NO. _____

IN THE MATTER OF THE MARRIAGE OF

_____ §

Petitioner [Print your full name]

AND §

_____ §

Respondent [Print your spouse's full name]

AND IN THE INTEREST OF §

MINOR CHILDREN: §

_____ §

_____ §

_____ §

_____ §

_____ §

_____ §

[Print the full names of your children]

IN THE DISTRICT COURT OF

COUNTY, TEXAS

#_____ JUDICIAL DISTRICT

> Fill out caption as shown on page 81

EMPLOYER'S ORDER TO WITHHOLD FROM EARNINGS FOR CHILD S

The Court ORDERS you, the employer of _____
to withhold income from the Obligor's disposable earnings from this employment as fo

OBLIGOR: *(the person who pays child support)*

Name: _____ Social security Number _____

Address: _____

OBLIGEE: *(the person who receives child support)*

Name: _____ Social security Number _____

Address: _____

> Information about the person who will be paying support, called the "obligor"

> Information about the person who will be receiving support, called the "obligee"

CHILDREN:

1. **Child's name** _____

Date of Birth: _____ Social Security #: _____

Date child turns 18 _____ Place of Birth: _____

> Note: You can omit your address if you fear to have your spouse know it.

Withholding Order

Page 1 of 5

Employer's Order to Withhold Earnings for Spousal Maintenance

Second page

Order to Withhold

The Court ORDERS employer to withhold the following amounts from the earnings of OBLIGOR:

(1) $_____ on current spousal maintenance, if OBLIGOR is paid monthly:

(2) $_____ on current spousal maintenance, if OBLIGOR is paid twice monthly:

(3) $_____ on current spousal maintenance, if OBLIGOR is paid every other week:

(4) $_____ on current spousal maintenance, if OBLIGOR is paid every week:

The Court ORDERS the employer to withhold the above amount until: _____

> You must put a number on all four lines. See note for how to calculate.

> Enter date or time period when support ends. See text note.

Calculating Disposable Earnings

The employer shall calculate OBLIGOR's disposable earnings, which are subject to withholding for child support, as follows:

1. Determine the "earnings" of OBLIGOR, which means compensation paid or payable for personal services, whether called wages, salary, compensation received as an independent contractor, overtime pay, severance pay, commission, bonus, or otherwise, including periodic payments pursuant to a pension, an annuity, workers' compensation, a disability and retirement program, and unemployment benefits;

2. Subtract the following sums to calculate OBLIGOR's "disposable earnings":
   a. any amounts required by law to be withheld, that is, federal income tax and federal FICA or OASI tax (Social Security) and Railroad Retirement Act contributions;
   b. union dues;
   c. nondiscretionary retirement contributions by OBLIGOR; and
   d. medical, hospitalization, and disability insurance coverage for OBLIGOR and OBLIGOR's children.

Notice of Change of Employment

The Court ORDERS the employer to notify the Court and OBLIGEE within seven days of the date that OBLIGOR terminates employment. The Court ORDERS the employer to provide OBLIGOR's last known address and the name and address of his new employer, if known.

Signed on _____

_____
Judge Presiding

Order to Withhold Earnings for Spousal Support   Page 2 of 2

E. How to fill out the Request to Issue Withholding Order

First of all, make a copy of the blank form to keep in your file. If the Obligor/Payor changes jobs in the future, you will need to fill out another one to have sent to the new employer.

Fill in the caption just like you did for all the other forms.

Fill in the blanks, as illustrated on the next page.

Privacy. In cases where you need to protect the location of a party, you can omit your place of residence, but will probably have to testify about your reasons.

Then what?

Make four copies of the form. You do not have to present these at the hearing, but keep them in your file anyway.

If you are going to order withholding for either child support or spousal maintenance at your first opportunity, then take this form to the clerk of the court right after the Decree and Withholding Order(s) are signed so the Withholding Order(s) can be served on the employer. You may have to pay a fee of $20 or so per order at this time.

If for some reason you are not going to ask the clerk to serve the order(s) on the employer right now, just keep this form in your file until the time comes that you do want the Withholding Order issued.

In all cases where children are receiving public assistance, the Withholding Order for child support *must* be issued by the clerk as soon as support is ordered in your Decree.

Request to Issue Withholding Order

Cause No._____

IN THE MATTER OF THE MARRIAGE OF: IN THE DISTRICT COURT

_____, Petitioner

                                                   ____ JUDICIAL DISTRICT
AND

_____, Respondent   _____ COUNTY, TEXAS

AND IN THE INTEREST OF _____

_____ MINOR CHILD(REN)

REQUEST TO ISSUE
EMPLOYER'S ORDER TO WITHHOLD
EARNINGS FOR CHILD SUPPORT OR SPOUSAL MAINTENANCE

To the Clerk of the Court:
    Please issue a certified copy of the following order in this cause:
        Order/Notice to Withhold from Earnings for Child Support,
        signed by the Court on _____ .

        Employer's Order to Withholding Earnings for Spousal Maintenance,
        signed by the Court on _____ .

And deliver the order to:
    Obligor's/Payor's Employer: _____
    Address: _____
    City, State, Zip: _____

Submitted on _____

Obligee/Payee

Address

> Fill out caption as shown on page 81.

> Indicate which Withholding Order you are requesting.

> Enter name and address of Payor's employer.

> Do not enter your address if you fear to have the Payor know it. See note.

10. The Military Affidavit

What it is

In every default case—that is, where Respondent has not filed a Response or a Waiver of Citation—you have to file a Military Affidavit with your Decree, stating under oath if you know whether or not Respondent is on active military duty.

If Respondent is on *active* duty and refuses to sign the Waiver, you will probably need to get an attorney to help you complete your case. Call Divorce Helpline for assistance.

If you have personal knowledge that Respondent is *not* on active duty, your job is done. Just check that box and get your statement notarized.

If you don't know for sure either way, you'll have to do some research to find out. Contact a local military office and ask their help, hire an investigator who specializes in finding information about people, dig around. List on your Affidavit what steps you have taken to determine that Respondent is or is not on active duty.

Your statements are made under penalty of perjury and must be notarized or signed in the presence of a court clerk who is authorized to take your statement under oath.

How to fill it out

Fill it out as shown in the illustrations on the next page.

Then what?

Sign the form under oath before either a Notary or clerk of the court. Make four copies and file along with your Decree.

Military Affidavit

Cause No._____

IN THE MATTER OF THE MARRIAGE OF: IN THE DISTRICT COUR

_____, Petitioner

                                                     ____ JUDICIAL DISTRICT

AND

_____, Respondent   _____ COUNTY, TEXAS

SERVICEMEMBERS CIVIL RELIEF ACT AFFIDAVIT

Affiant, being duly sworn on his/her oath deposes and says under penalty of perjury that:

I am ☐ Petitioner   ☐ Petitioner's agent in the above entitled matter.

I have ☐   personal knowledge that Respondent is not in the military on active duty.
       ☐   made a personal investigation of records of the United States military.
       ☐   researched the following internet military site _____
           to discover whether Respondent is in the military.
       ☐   researched whether Respondent is in the military from the following sources:

           _____

Based upon the foregoing, it is my belief that

       ☐   the above-named Respondent is **not** in the military service on active duty.
       ☐   the above-named Respondent is in the military service on active duty.
       ☐   I have been unable to determine whether or not the defendant is in the military service
           on active duty.

I understand that statements in this document are made under penalty of perjury and that making a false statement is a violation of Federal Law and is subject to both fine and imprisonment.

_____
Affiant

Subscribed and sworn to before me this _____ Day of _____, 200__

                                   _____
                                   Notary public in and for the state of Texas
                                   or Officer Authorized to Administer Oaths
                                   or Clerk of the Court   (strike all but one)

Military Affidavit   Page 1 of 1

Fill out caption as shown on page 81

Indicate which party you are in the case.

Indicate how you know about Respondent's military status.

Indicate your belief about Respondent's military status.

Sign before a Notary or other authorized person.

11. The Hearing

In order to complete your divorce, and as the *last* (hooray!) item of business, you must attend a hearing and say a few words about your case. The hearing will be very brief, almost a mere formality. Most of your time will be spent waiting for it to start, and it will be over in a few minutes. So don't worry. In the next few pages, we show you how to set the date, what to do when you get there, and what to say. It is very unlikely that you will have any problems, but we have instructions to cover even that rare event.

A. Are you ready? Prehearing checklist

1. All cases

There is a 60-day waiting period, which is required in all cases. It can sometimes be quite tricky to compute, so it is safe to allow two months and two weeks to pass from the date you filed your Petition before the day of your hearing.

2. Waiver cases

If your spouse signed the Waiver form, and it is properly signed, notarized, and on file at the District Clerk's Office, then you can set the hearing as soon as the two-months-plus-two-weeks waiting period is over.

Make sure you have your Decree, the Withholding Order (if your Decree orders child support), and the Information on Suit Affecting Family Relationship form completed before you go in. If you plan to have your spouse's signature on the Decree or any other written agreements, this must be done before you go in for the hearing.

3. Default cases

Before you have your hearing:

a) At least two months plus two weeks must have passed since the date you filed your Petition, *and*

b) At least 27 days must have passed since the date your spouse was served with papers, *and*

c) At least 12 days must have passed since the date the Officer's Return (on the Citation) was filed with the District Clerk's Office.

B. Getting into court

The way uncontested divorces are scheduled varies from county to county. It is usually informal, and always easy to do. When you are ready to set the date, call the District Clerk's Office and ask for the clerk of your court (give the number of the District Court that appears in the caption of your documents). Ask the clerk when uncontested divorce hearings are scheduled and also ask if they want any advance notice, either by phone or in writing, of when you will be coming in for your hearing.

Ask the clerk how the court's file for your case will get to the courtroom at the proper time. In some counties, you go into the District Clerk's Office ahead of the hearing and get your own file and carry it to the courtroom yourself. In other counties, you notify the clerk ahead of time when you are coming in for your hearing, and they send it to court for you.

We strongly recommend, some time before you have your own hearing, that you go into your courtroom as a spectator to watch other uncontested divorces. This will give you a very good idea of what will happen in your own case, and how your judge runs his or her courtroom. It will help you get ready for your own case. The Clerk's Office can tell you when uncontested divorces are heard by your court.

C. The day of the hearing

Get to the courthouse a little before your case is scheduled. Unless your county is one where the clerk does it for you, you should get your file from the District Clerk's Office, take it to your courtroom, and hand it to the bailiff (the guy with the uniform) or the clerk. Whether or not you are delivering a file, you should go up to the clerk or bailiff and let them know you are present and ready. Have a seat among the spectators and wait for your case to be called.

When your case is called, you answer "ready" and go up before the judge. The judge will administer the oath, then tell you to proceed. In some courts you stand before the judge's bench, and in others you will take the witness stand. The judge will indicate which you are to do. In either case, take time to arrange your papers and your notes, relax, and give your testimony. Always refer to the judge as "Your Honor" and don't lean on the bench if you are standing before it.

In some counties, a family law "master" or "referee" will hear the case. A master is a judge who is appointed by other judges, rather than elected. They have most of the duties of an elected judge, but their decisions must be approved by an elected judge. This will not be a problem for most people, especially if you have an agreed or default divorce. If the master asks you if you object to having him/her hear the case, say no. A master is called "Your Honor" just like an elected judge. If the master makes a ruling you disagree with, you have three days to ask an elected judge to review the master's decision.

If you are asked, state that you are willing to waive the presence of the court reporter. There is no particular advantage to having a word-for-word record of an uncontested divorce, and it is very expensive to make.

Your testimony will cover the basic facts of your case, the circumstances of your marriage, and what you are asking the court to do. It runs exactly parallel to your Petition, and what you ask for must match what is in your Decree.

The outline below is not exactly what you must say, but rather it is a guide to help you order your testimony. It wouldn't be good to take this book to court and read from it, so we put the guide on the CD in the Forms Etc folder so you can print it out. Or you can type or write notes from these pages. Check off each item as you give it in court, and don't skip or forget to say any part of it. Take your time, relax. If the judge asks questions, it is only because s/he is trying to make sure that things are being done fairly and correctly. Don't worry, just answer *briefly* and *exactly* the question asked. Don't volunteer information the judge does not ask for.

A Guide for Your Testimony*

* This guide is also found on the companion CD in the Testimony folder, so you can easily print it and take it with you.

I. In every case, give the following information

A. Your Honor, my name is _____, and I am the Petitioner in this case.

B. All of the facts stated in the Petition are true.

C. At the time of filing of this Petition, I had been continually a resident of Texas for more than six months, and of this county for more than 90 days.

D. I am now married to _____, who is the Respondent in this case. We were married on ____(date)_____, and we separated on ___(date) ____, and have not lived together as husband and wife since that time. (These dates must be the same as those given in the Petition. For common-law marriages, the language in the Petition is your guide for what to say at this point.)

E. I am seeking this divorce because our marriage has become insupportable due to discord or conflict of personalities, which has destroyed the legitimate ends of our marriage relationship. There is no chance for a reconciliation. Your Honor, I request that this marriage be dissolved. Would Your Honor like me to go into the particular circumstances of our marriage that led to this request for a divorce?

(If the judge says to do so, give a *brief* statement as to why your marriage cannot continue. Do not emphasize fault or blame, but describe differences, arguing, conflict, personality clashes, and so on. Tell about efforts to save the marriage. If there was any, describe violence, cruelty, drug abuse, abandonment, failure to support, neglect by your spouse. Conclude by stating that there is no possibility for a reconciliation.)

II. Continue, using the portions that apply to your case

A. The Decree and Agreements

Hand the Decree to the judge and state, "Your Honor, here is the Decree that I have prepared and that I am submitting to you at this time."

- If your spouse signed the Decree, state, "This Decree has been approved by my spouse, whose signature is on the last page. I am familiar with the signature of my spouse and can state that it is genuine."

- If there is a written agreement, hand the *original* and a copy to the judge at this time and state, "Here is the original and a copy of a written agreement between my spouse and myself. I am familiar with the signature of my spouse and can state that it is genuine. I request that the copy of the agreement be admitted into evidence and that the original be returned to me at the end of this hearing."

B. Children

1. **None.** Your Honor, my spouse and I have no minor, unmarried children, and none are expected.

2. **If You Have Children**

   If child custody and support are part of a written agreement, tell the judge, "The written agreement before Your Honor's consideration contains provisions concerning the custody and support of the child(ren)."

   In every case, tell the court:

   a) Your Honor, the Respondent and myself are the parents of (a) child(ren). (Give name, age, birth date, and birthplace for each). Apart from personal possessions, no property is owned by the child(ren).

   b) **Jurisdiction.** State one of the following:

   • The Respondent is a resident of Texas, or

   • The Respondent is not a resident of Texas, but:
   (State the best reasons that apply to your case from the list under "The parent/child long arm" in Chapter A, section 6(b).)

   c) **Custody.** State one of the following:

   • It would be in the best interest of the child(ren) for Respondent and I to be named Joint Managing Conservators.

   • It would be in the best interest of the child(ren) if (I/Respondent) were to have the care, custody, and control of the child(ren). The child(ren) live(s) with (me/Respondent) at this time, and (is/are) being well cared for. I am asking the court to name (me/my spouse) as Managing Conservator. (Be prepared to explain why this arrangement is better than Joint Managing Conservatorship.)

   d) **Possession Schedule**
   Your Honor, it would be best for the children if the schedule for possession were to be ordered (state one of the following)

   • **Standard terms:** for the specified times and places as set forth in the proposed Decree and the attached schedule, which is in substantial compliance with the Texas state standard for possession of minors.

- **Major departure from the standard terms:** for the specified times and places as set forth in the proposed Decree and the attached schedule. Your Honor, the reasons for requesting this particular schedule for possession are as follows (give reasons with any supporting evidence).

e) **Support:** Be prepared to testify to the income and earning ability of both spouses and the custodial parent's expenses. Optional: use the Financial Information form in the back of this book as a guide, take it to the hearing for reference, or submit it to the judge if he or she asks a lot of questions.

Your Honor, (I am/my spouse is) able to earn a living and pay reasonable support for the child(ren). (State details or submit Financial Form.) I am requesting that (I/my spouse) be ordered to pay (state terms you set out in Decree). I also request that the court sign the attached Withholding Order.

f) **Class Attendance** (if required in your county):

- Your Honor, my spouse and I have completed the class required for parents. Here are the original certificates to be filed with the court.

    or

- Your Honor, I have completed the class required for parents. I have my certificate of completion to be filed with the court. I was unable to find my spouse to have him/her take the course. I request that you waive the requirement that my spouse take this class.

g) **Handicapped Child:** (Name of child) has a disability and requires continuous care and personal supervision and will not be capable of self-support. I request that payments for the support of this child be continued past the child's 18th birthday and extended for an indefinite period.

h) **Spousal Maintenance:** I am requesting that spousal maintenance be ordered. (State the qualifying grounds and the reason you need the support. Show the judge your Financial Form to back up your figures.)

C. Property and Debts

1. None. Your Honor, there is no community property of any significant value apart from our personal effects.

2. Approved Decree: Your Honor, the Respondent and I have agreed to the division of property and debts as set forth in the Decree, and Respondent has signed the last page of that Decree. (Using your Petition as a guide, recite your community property and debts, and any separate property, then indicate which property and debts you wish the court to award to you and which to your spouse.)

3. Written Contract. The division of our community property and debts is covered by the written contract that I have submitted for Your Honor's approval. I request that you approve our agreement and incorporate it into the Decree.

4. Divided by the Court. Your Honor, there is some property in this case that should be fairly divided by order of this court.

- During the marriage, we accumulated certain property, which is listed in the Petition. (Using your Petition as a guide, recite the property listed.)

- There is also certain separate property, which is listed in the Petition, and which should be confirmed as separate property. (Recite the property, using the Petition as your guide.)

- Your Honor, there are certain circumstances that make it fair that a large share of the property be awarded to (Petitioner/Respondent). (Recite the circumstances: custody of children requiring house and furniture, needs of one, earning ability of other, special circumstances, and so on.)

- Your Honor, it is requested that the following division of property and debts be ordered: (Recite your request, following the terms of your prepared Decree.)

D. Change Of Name

Your Honor, (I/Respondent) desire(s) and request(s) that (my/his/her) name be changed to ___(give desired name in full)___. As of September 1, 1995, a judge can no longer refuse to change your name back to one you formerly used just because it would give you a different last name than your children.

E. Conclusion

State, "Your Honor, that concludes my testimony."

The judge may ask further questions, which you should answer briefly, sticking just to the point he asked about.

In almost all cases, the judge will announce the orders, sign your Decree, and you may go. You are finished. Divorced. It is over. Congratulations! Collect your papers, take all copies of the Decree to the clerk of your court, and get them stamped. Minor adjustments may be made by the clerk on the spot, but if the judge's orders were very different from your prepared Decree, you may have to make up a new Decree conforming exactly to the judge's orders, and present it for signing and stamping at a later time. Do it as soon as possible.

D. Troubleshooting Guide

We said it before and say it again: 99 times out of 100 there will be no trouble with the hearing. However, it will make you feel better if you know what to do just in case you are that unfortunate one.

1. Before the hearing begins

It sometimes happens that the people who work in the court forget who pays their salaries—that is, you and the other taxpayers. It usually does no good to remind them. Rather, if the clerk or the bailiff (or even the judge) is not helpful or polite, just keep calm, be polite, and firmly pursue your point. You have a right to represent yourself.

If someone is obstructing your way, it is very possible that there is a reason. If so, you must find it out and correct the problem. Ask what is the matter; at least get them to indicate the general area of the problem, or give you some hints as to the reason for their action or conduct. If necessary, ask to speak to another clerk, or to the supervisor. Don't get upset—the only important thing is for you to figure out and correct any errors in your papers or procedures. Go over this book and double-check everything. You can always come back to the Clerk's Office or to court another day.

2. After your hearing begins

This is a scary time for something to go wrong, but don't worry, you have an excellent escape hatch (or panic button) that you can use if all else fails. It is called the continuance. Lawyers use it all the time.

If things go very wrong and you can't figure out what your problem is, or how to solve it, or if you get into any kind of situation you can't handle, just tell the judge,

"Your Honor, I respectfully request that this matter be continued to another date so that I may have time to seek advice and further prepare this case for presentation." This way, you can come back another day, giving you time to try to find out what went wrong, or maybe ask to see the judge in chambers. Perhaps the judge will talk to you about it. It's worth a try. In any case, go over this book very carefully to see if you left anything out.

If the judge refuses to grant your divorce at the end of your testimony, this means he or she is not satisfied with some portion of it; it was probably incomplete, something left out. Ask the judge, politely, to please explain his or her reasons, as it may be that you can give additional testimony that will solve the problem. If the judge indicates which portion of your case is incomplete, go over it again, more carefully and fully. If the judge will not help or explain, ask to have your case continued to another day. During the recess, see if the clerk or bailiff will help you, or ask to see the judge in chambers. Go over this book and double-check everything.

Assuming you find out what went wrong, go in for another hearing, and try it again.

3. After the hearing

If the judge grants your divorce but refuses to sign your Decree, then this probably means the judge thinks something is wrong with it. Probably it is different from the orders announced in court. The divorce is still valid and effective, but your case will not be over and complete until you can prepare a Decree that the judge will sign. Ask the judge what is wrong, and make careful note of the explanation. Ask the clerk. Look at the clerk's docket sheet (it's a public record) where notes are entered as to the orders in your case. Make up a new Decree and bring it in at another time, but do it as soon as possible.

Appendix A

Affidavit of Inability to Pay

Rule 145 of the Texas Rules of Civil Procedure guarantees that no low-income Texan will be denied access to the courts simply because he or she cannot afford to pay the court costs. A party who is unable to afford costs is defined as "a person who is presently receiving a governmental entitlement based on indigency or any other person who has no ability to pay costs."

Anyone receiving public assistance automatically qualifies under this rule.

The law does not contain guidelines for exactly how much income people not receiving public assistance can have and still qualify for the pauper's oath, but you would have to show that you can't pay for the essentials of life and also pay court fees. If you think you might qualify, go ahead and try it. The worst thing that can happen is they will decide you don't qualify.

The two-page form, "Affidavit of Inability," is found at the back and on the CD that comes with this book. Fill it out as completely as possible, checking all relevant boxes. Sign it before a Notary Public and file it at the same time that you file your Petition.

Appendix B
Special Custody Rules for Military Personnel

Texas law has long been sensitive to the needs of military personnel with minor children. There is now a revised plan, described below, that affects cases filed on or after September 1, 2009. After you read this appendix, if you want help with understanding these rules or how to apply them to your case, check to see if your military unit offers counseling and legal advice services for personnel and their families, otherwise call Divorce Helpline.

The new plan covers two situations: (A) when a military parent is ordered away, and (B) when a military parent returns from deployment. Family Code §153.3162 and §153.701–153.709.

A. When a military parent is ordered away—temporary court orders

If a military parent is ordered to deployment, mobilization, or temporary duty that involves moving a substantial distance from the child's residence so as to materially affect the parent's ability to exercise parental rights and duties, either parent can request a temporary order to revise custody or visitation or child support. This temporary order will terminate on the return of the military parent to his/her usual residence.

The Home Parent. If the affected military parent is the Home Parent—the parent with the exclusive right to designate the primary residence of the child—the court can appoint another person to exercise the right to designate the child's primary residence during the military parent's absence. This can be the Co-Parent, but if that is not in the child's best interest, another person can be named. At the court's discretion, the designated person can have some or all of the same rights and duties as the absent military parent.

If the court appoints the Co-Parent to act for Home-Parent in Home-Parent's absence, the court can appoint a person named by the Home-Parent to have visitation rights in the Home-Parent's absence. The visitation schedule will be the same as was exercised by the Co-Parent before the Home-Parent was ordered away, except that the court can expand or limit these rights as it finds to be in the best interests of the child.

The Co-Parent. If the affected military parent is the Co-Parent—the parent who does not have the exclusive right to designate the primary residence of the child—and if the court finds it is in the best interests of the child, the court can award visitation to a person chosen by the Co-Parent. The visitation schedule will be the same as was exercised by the Co-Parent before the Co-Parent was ordered away, except that the court can expand or limit these rights as it finds to be in the best interests of the child.

Enforcement. Temporary orders can be enforced by or against the designated person to the same extent and manner as would be the case for the military parent.

Temporary order for child support. If being ordered away has a material effect on the military parent's ability to pay child support, the military parent can request an expedited (faster than normal) hearing at which it is possible to request that testimony and evidence be given by electronic means, including teleconferencing.

B. When a military parent returns from deployment

If a Co-Parent or Joint Managing Conservator was deployed to a location where access to the child was not reasonably possible, on return from deployment that parent has up to 90 days to petition the court for additional care time to make up for contact with the child that was lost due to the military deployment. The court has broad discretion to consider all circumstances and determine whether and how much additional care time is in the best interest of the child. If additional care time is ordered, when it has been exercised, all parties return to the orders they were under before the military deployment.

Appendix C

How to Fill Out the Special Warranty Deed

A special warranty deed is included with the forms in the back of this book. It transfers title from one party to the other, without the party who is giving away the property guaranteeing that the chain of title is correct. If a title insurance policy was involved in the original purchase of the house and you and your spouse have not assigned away any part of your property to other parties during the marriage, you have nothing to worry about. If you purchased your house without a title policy, you may wish to contact a title company to verify that there are no "clouds" on the title, particularly if you are the person receiving the house. A title search generally costs about $100.

Do not use this deed form if you are not transferring property between spouses. It has specialized language regarding the transfer that is not applicable to a general sale of land. Consult an attorney or call Divorce Helpline if you have questions about other types of deeds.

Either fill in the blanks with a typewriter or retype this special warranty deed on a letter-size piece of paper. It is okay if the deed runs over to a second page.

The "Grantor" is the person giving the property and the "Grantee" is the person receiving the property.

1. Type in Grantor's name and name of county where Grantor resides.

2. Copy the cause number and style (caption) of the case as it appears on your Original Petition or Divorce Decree. If you have children, you will have to add the "And in the Interest of _____ Child(ren)" block as on your other papers. That would definitely mean typing the whole warranty deed over.

   If you are filing the deed *before* you file the divorce petition, you don't need any of the court information on lines 5 to 7. Draw lines through all this, starting on line 4 with "namely the division of property in:" and ending with "Judicial District Court of _____ County, Texas."

3. Type in Grantee's name and name of county where Grantee resides.

4. Type the property description *exactly* as it appears on the warranty deed you received when you bought the property. It is extremely important that you list it in the same way it is spelled out, otherwise the transfer of title might be defective and cause problems later on. If you have a very long description (like a surveyor's sheet that runs for a page or more), you may

want to photocopy it, attach it to the back page of the deed, and call it "Exhibit A." If so, type "See Exhibit A." in this space.

5. Skip the rest of the blanks for the moment and type in Grantee's name and address on the bottom left side of the deed.

6. The Grantor must now take the warranty deed to a Notary Public, and sign and date it in the Notary's presence. The Notary Public fills in the rest of the blank lines.

After this is all done, the deed must be filed with the county clerk in the county where the property is located. There is a nominal filing fee, usually $5 for the first page and $3 for each successive page. *The deed must be filed with the county clerk in order to be valid.*

Order of the Forms*

CD #	Title
01	Original Petition for Divorce
01-A	Child Information
02	Waiver of Citation
03	Citations (two: within county and without county)
04	Information for Service of Process
05	Final Decree of Divorce
05-Ex1	Children's Property
05-Ex2	Conservatorship Order
05-Ex3	Standard Possession Order
05-Ex4	Child Support Order
05-Ex5	Health Insurance Order
05-Ex6	Required Information
05-Ex7	Orders Re Property and Debts
06	Statistics Form
07	Order/Notice to Withhold Income for Child Support
08	Employer's Order to Withhold Earnings for Spousal Maintenance
09	Request to Issue Withholding Order
10	Military Affidavit
11	Financial Information
12	Affidavit of Inability to Pay
13	Power of Attorney to Transfer Motor Vehicle
14	Special Warranty Deed (to Transfer Real Property)

Additional Forms etc. on the Companion CD

01-B	Travis Standing Order
07A	Chapter 158 of Family Code
MSA	Marital Settlement Agreement
	2009 Tax Charts
	Property Checklist
	Testimony Guide
Kits	Citations by Publication or Posting
	Motion to Consolidate

* Remember, you don't use all of these forms—only the ones you need for your case.

IN THE MATTER OF THE MARRIAGE OF:

_____, Petitioner

AND

_____, Respondent

AND IN THE INTEREST OF _____

_____ **MINOR CHILD(REN)**

IN THE DISTRICT COURT

____ **JUDICIAL DISTRICT**

_____ **COUNTY, TEXAS**

ORIGINAL PETITION FOR DIVORCE

1. **Parties and Discovery**

    This suit is brought by Petitioner, _____, who resides at

    _____

    Respondent is _____, who resides at

    _____

    ☐ Discovery Level 1 applies to this case as there are no minor children of the marriage whose custody and support will be determined, the wife is not pregnant, **and** the value of the marital estate that we currently own is not more than $50,000.00.

    ☐ Discovery Level 2 applies to this case because ☐ there are minor children of the marriage whose custody and support will be determined and/or ☐ the value of the marital estate that we currently own is more than $50,000.00.

2. **Residency (Domicile)**

    ☐ Petitioner ☐ Respondent has been a domiciliary of the State of Texas for the preceding six months and a resident of the county in which this petition is filed for the preceding ninety days.

3. Service of Process

☐ **Waiver.** No service is necessary at this time because Respondent has signed or will sign a Waiver of Service. If my spouse does not sign a Waiver of Service, I will ask a sheriff or constable to give a copy of this Original Petition for Divorce to Respondent at the following address:

_____.

☐ Process should be served on Respondent at the following address:

_____.

4. Protective Order Statement

☐ There is no protective order between the parties and no application for one is pending.

☐ A protective order is presently in effect or an application for protective order is pending at this time in the _____ Court, _____ County, Texas, Cause No. _____. A true and correct copy of the protective order
    ☐ is attached to this Original Petition.
    ☐ is unavailable now but will be filed with the court before any hearings in this case.

5. Marriage and Separation

☐ Petitioner and Respondent were married on or about _____, _____, and ceased to live together as husband and wife on or about _____, _____.

☐ Common-Law Marriage: Petitioner and Respondent agreed to be married on or about _____, _____, and thereafter lived together in Texas as husband and wife and there represented to others that they were married, thus creating a common-law marriage. The parties separated on or about _____, _____.

6. Grounds

The marriage has become insupportable because of discord or conflict of personalities that destroys the legitimate ends of the marriage relationship and prevents any reasonable expectation of reconciliation.

7. Community Property (including debts) (Check only one box)

☐ **No property.** To Petitioner's knowledge, other than personal effects there is no community property of any significant value which is subject to division by the Court at this time.

☐ **Divided by agreement.** Petitioner believes the parties will reach an agreed property division and ask the Court to approve that agreement when presented to the Court or, absent agreement, divide the assets and debts of the parties according to Texas law.

☐ **Marital Settlement Agreement.** The parties have entered into a Marital Settlement Agreement, a copy of which is attached and incorporated by reference.

☐ **Divided by Court.**

    (1) **Itemization:** To Petitioner's knowledge, the community property owned by the parties consists of the following assets and debts:

Item #	Description	Value

    (2) **Division:** Petitioner requests the Court to order a division of the property in a manner that the Court deems just and right, as provided by law.

☐ It would be fair to divide the property into approximately equal portions.

☐ There are many equities which the court should consider making it fair that

    ☐ Petitioner ☐ Respondent be awarded a substantial portion of the property.

☐ It will be fair and equitable for the Court to order Respondent to assume and to pay without any right to contribution or reimbursement from Petitioner the debts described in the above list at items numbered: _____

Original Petition for Divorce

8. Separate Property

☐ I request that the following items be confirmed as Petitioner's separate property as they were owned before the marriage or acquired during marriage by inheritance, gift to Petitioner only, or represents the proceeds, other than lost wages, of a personal injury lawsuit:

☐ I request that the following items be confirmed as Respondent's separate property as they were owned before the marriage or acquired during marriage by inheritance, gift to Respondent only, or represents the proceeds, other than lost wages, of a personal injury lawsuit:

9. Spousal Maintenance

☐ Maintenance is not requested.

☐ Petitioner requests that this court award maintenance for the following reasons:

   ☐ Petitioner and Respondent were married at least 10 years.
   ☐ Respondent was convicted of or received deferred adjudication for a family violence crime within two years from the date of the filing of this Petition.

In addition to the above, Petitioner lacks sufficient property, including property distributed after this divorce, to provide for Petitioner's minimum reasonable needs; and Petitioner

   ☐ clearly lacks the earning ability in the labor market adequate to provide for Petitioner's minimum reasonable needs.
   ☐ is unable to support him/herself through employment because of an incapacitating physical or mental disability.
   ☐ is the custodian of a child who requires substantial care and personal supervision because of a physical or mental disability which makes it necessary that Petitioner not be employed outside of the home.

10. Change of Name

☐ No change of name is requested.

☐ It is requested that the Court order a change of name for _____ and that the name be changed to _____

11. Children of the Marriage

The wife is not pregnant.

☐ No unmarried children now under eighteen years of age were born to or adopted by the parties of the marriage. We do not have any children who are 18 years or older who are disabled. We do not have children together who are in need of child or medical support.

☐ The following children now under eighteen years old were born to or adopted by the parties:

Name	Age	Sex	Birth date	Birthplace
1.				
2.				
3.				
4.				
5.				

☐ _____, a child of this marriage, requires continuous care and personal supervision because of a disability and will not be capable of self-support. The Court is requested to order that payments for the support of this child be continued after the child's eighteenth birthday and extended for an indefinite period.

Children's Property. No property, aside from personal effects is owned by the children above
☐ except as listed here:

☐ The husband is NOT the biological father of these children born during the marriage:

Name	Age	Sex	Birth date	Birthplace
1.				
2.				

Information required by Texas Family Code § 152.209   (check one box)
☐ Is not required because both parents reside in Texas.
☐ Is submitted in an attached affidavit as Exhibit A.
☐ Is not provided because the health, safety, or liberty of a party or child would be jeopardized by disclosure of identifying information.

Private health care coverage   (choose one below)
☐ is currently in effect for the child(ren) under policy number _____ with the
_____ insurance company, and _____ is responsible for paying the premium of _____ per month. Said insurance is/is not provided through employment.

☐ There is currently no private health care coverage in effect for the child(ren) and

☐ the child(ren) is/are not receiving health care under any public health care program.

☐ the child(ren) is/are receiving health care under the following public health care
program(s): _____

Court of Continuing Jurisdiction (check one box)

☐ No other person has a court-ordered right to be notified about this divorce. No court ordered relationship exists between the children and any other person. No other court has continuing, exclusive jurisdiction over any child in the above list.

☐ The above named children are under the continuing, exclusive jurisdiction of the _____ Judicial District of _____ County, in the state of _____, in Cause Number _____. A final order has been entered in that case, establishing custody, child support, and visitation and Petitioner does not wish to make any changes to the prior order.

Conservatorship (Custody), Possession and Support

Upon final hearing,

☐ Petitioner and Respondent should be appointed Joint Managing Conservators of the child(ren) and _____ should have the right to establish the child(ren)'s primary residence.

☐ _____ should be appointed the Sole Managing Conservator of the child(ren) and _____ should be appointed Possessory Conservator of the child(ren).

Possession should be arranged according to the best interests of the child(ren).

☐ Petitioner ☐ Respondent should be ordered to make payments for the support of the children in the manner specified by the Court.

12. **Long-arm Jurisdiction:** Respondent is not a resident of Texas, but this court may exercise personal jurisdiction over him/her because: (check all that apply)

☐ Texas is the last state where the parties lived together as husband and wife and it has been less than two years since we separated.

☐ Respondent agrees this Court may exercise personal jurisdiction over him/her.

☐ The above child(ren) (was/were) conceived in Texas and Respondent is a parent.

☐ Respondent resided in Texas and provided prenatal expenses and/or support for the child(ren).

☐ Respondent resided with the child(ren) in Texas

☐ The child(ren) reside(s) in Texas as a result of the acts or directives or with the approval of the Respondent.

13. Personal Information (check one box)

☐ In the Final Decree of Divorce, I will include the Social Security and driver's license numbers, current addresses, and phone numbers for each party and child who is subject to this suit, as required by section 105.006 of the Texas Family Code.

☐ I ask the Court to seal any attachment to the Final Decree, and any Orders to Withhold Earnings that the court might issue, that disclose the Social Security and driver's license numbers, current address, and telephone numbers of parties or children in order to protect parties and children from exposure to identity theft. Such information will be provided to parties and the court but should not be made part of files to which the public has access.

☐ I ask the Court's permission not to disclose the Social Security and driver's license numbers, current address, and telephone numbers in the Final Decree of Divorce because providing that information is likely to cause the child or a parent harassment, abuse, serious harm, or injury.

PRAYER

☐ Petitioner prays that citation and notice be given to Respondent as required by law.

Petitioner prays that the Court grant a divorce and decree such other relief as is requested in this petition.

Petitioner prays for such other and further relief, general and special, to which Petitioner may be entitled.

Dated: _____, 20___.

_____
Petitioner, Pro Se

Address _____

_____

Phone: _____

Attachment(s) to this Petition:
☐ Exhibit A. Information Re Minors Required Under §152.209, Texas Family Code
☐ Copy of Protective Order described in item 4 above   (if applicable)
☐ Travis County Standing Order Regarding Children, Property and Conduct of Parties
(if case filed in Travis County)

EXHIBIT ___. INFORMATION REQUIRED BY TEXAS FAMILY CODE § 152.209

STATE OF TEXAS
COUNTY OF _____

BEFORE ME, the undersigned authority, on this day personally appeared
_____, who being by me duly sworn, on oath stated:

1. My name is _____. I am Petitioner, representing myself in this proceeding to determine the custody of the following children whose present addresses, places of residence over the past five years, and names and addresses of persons with whom they lived during that period are as follows:

2. _____, age ___, who lived from _____ to _____ the present with ☐ Petitioner ☐ Respondent ☐ Other: _____
whose current address is _____

And from _____ to _____, resided at _____
with _____, whose current address is _____

And from _____ to _____, resided at _____
with _____, whose current address is _____

And from _____ to _____, resided at _____
with _____, whose current address is _____

3. _____, age ___, who lived from _____ to _____ present with ☐ Petitioner ☐ Respondent ☐ Other: _____
whose current address is _____

And from _____ to _____, resided at _____
with _____, whose current address is _____

And from _____ to _____, resided at _____
with _____, whose current address is _____

And from _____ to _____, resided at _____
with _____, whose current address is _____

4. _____, age ___, who lived from _____ to present with ☐ Petitioner ☐ Respondent ☐ Other: _____ whose current address is _____

And from _____ to _____, resided at _____ with _____, whose current address is _____

And from _____ to _____, resided at _____ with _____, whose current address is _____

And from _____ to _____, resided at _____ with _____, whose current address is _____

5. _____, age ___, who lived from _____ to present with ☐ Petitioner ☐ Respondent ☐ Other: _____ whose current address is _____

And from _____ to _____, resided at _____ with _____, whose current address is _____

And from _____ to _____, resided at _____ with _____, whose current address is _____

And from _____ to _____, resided at _____ with _____, whose current address is _____

6. _____, age ___, who lived from _____ to present with ☐ Petitioner ☐ Respondent ☐ Other: _____ whose current address is _____

And from _____ to _____, resided at _____ with _____, whose current address is _____

And from _____ to _____, resided at _____ with _____, whose current address is _____

And from _____ to _____, resided at _____ with _____, whose current address is _____

7. I have not participated, as a party or witness or in any other capacity, in any other proceeding concerning the custody of or visitation with the child(ren)

    ☐ except as follows: (identify court, case number, and date of any child custody determination)

8. I do not know of any proceeding that could affect the current proceeding, including proceedings for enforcement, domestic violence, protective orders, termination of parental rights, and adoption

☐ except as follows: (identify court, case number, and nature of the proceeding)

9. I do not know the names and addresses of any person not a party to the current proceeding who has physical custody of the child or claims rights of legal custody or physical custody of, or visitation with, the child(ren)

☐ except as follows: (give names and addresses of those persons)

10. I understand that I have a continuing duty to inform the court of any proceeding in this or any other state that could affect the current proceeding.

☐ **Request that this information be sealed.**
I believe that the health, safety, or liberty of myself or a child would be jeopardized by disclosure of identifying information, for the following reasons:

and therefore request the court to ORDER the information to be sealed and not be disclosed to the other party or the public unless the court orders the disclosure to be made after a hearing in which the court takes into consideration the health, safety, or liberty of myself or a child and determines that the disclosure is in the interest of justice.

Signed under oath on this ___ day of _____, 20__.

_____
Petitioner, Pro Se

SUBSCRIBED AND SWORN to before me this ___ day of_____, 20__.

_____
Notary Public, State of Texas
or Officer Authorized to Administer Oaths

Cause Number _____

IN THE MATTER OF THE MARRIAGE OF: IN THE DISTRICT COURT

_____, **Petitioner**

AND   ____ **JUDICIAL DISTRICT**

_____, **Respondent**   _____ **COUNTY, TEXAS**

AND IN THE INTEREST OF _____

_____ **MINOR CHILD(REN)**

WAIVER OF CITATION

THE STATE OF TEXAS
COUNTY OF _____

On this day, _____ personally appeared before me, the undersigned authority, who being duly sworn by me, upon oath says:

I, _____, am the Respondent in this case. My address is _____

I have received a file-stamped copy of the Original Petition for Divorce which I have read and understand.

☐ I have also been given a copy of the Travis County Standing Order Regarding Children, Property and Conduct of Parties, which takes affect automatically, and which I have read and understand.

I hereby enter my appearance in said cause for all purposes, waive the issuance, service and return of Citation upon me, and agree that said cause may be taken up and considered by the Court at any time without further notice to me. I agree that this case may be heard by a duly appointed master or referee of this court. I waive the making of a record of testimony.

I agree that the Judge can finalize my divorce without asking me about my side of the facts, without my signature on the Final Decree of Divorce, and without further notice to me.

I hereby waive all rights, privileges and exemptions, including appointment of counsel, pursuant to the Soldier's and Sailor's Civil Relief Act of 1940.

☐ I am not requesting a name change.

☐ I am requesting my name be returned to the following name that I used before I was married:

_____

/s/ _____
                          Respondent

Address _____

_____

Phone: _____

SWORN TO and SUBSCRIBED before me

on this _____ day of _____, 20___, to certify which witness my hand and seal of office.

I hereby certify that I am not an attorney in this case.

/s/ _____
                    Notary Public
          or Officer Authorized to Administer Oaths

THE STATE OF TEXAS   (Respondent Within the County)

Notice to Defendant: You have been sued. You may employ an attorney. If you or your attorney do not file a written answer with the clerk who issued this citation by 10:00 a.m. on the Monday next following the expiration of twenty days after you were served this citation and petition, a default judgment may be taken against you.

TO: _____ Defendant, Greeting:

You are hereby commanded to appear by filing a written answer to the Plaintiff's Petition at or before ten o'clock a.m. of the Monday next after the expiration of twenty days after the date of service of this citation before the ____ District Court of _____ County, Texas, at the courthouse of said County in the City of _____, Texas.

Said Plaintiff's Petition was filed in said court on the ____ day of _____, 20___, in this case, numbered _____, and styled

_____, Petitioner, and _____, Respondent.

The nature of Petitioner's demand is fully shown by a true and correct copy of the Petition accompanying this citation and made a part hereof.

The officer executing this writ shall promptly serve the same according to requirements of law, and the mandates thereof, and make due return as the law directs. Issued and given under my hand and seal of said Court at _____, Texas, this ____ day of _____, 20___,

Attest: _____

Clerk, District Court, _____ County, Texas

By _____, Deputy.

OFFICER'S RETURN

The within citation came to hand on the ____ day of _____. 20___, at _____ o'clock (am)(pm), and was by me executed at _____, within the county of _____, at _____ o'clock (am)(pm), on the ____ day of _____, 20___, by delivering to the within named _____ in person, a true copy of this citation, having first endorsed thereon the date of delivery, together with the accompanying true and correct copy of the Petition.

Sheriff's Fee............ $_____

| **Sheriff Account** |
| No. _____ |

To certify which witness my hand officially: _____

_____

Sheriff of _____ County, Texas

By _____, Deputy

| **For Clerk's Use** |
| Taxed _____ |
| Return recorded _____ |

THE STATE OF TEXAS

(Respondent Without the County)

Notice to Defendant: You have been sued. You may employ an attorney. If you or your attorney do not file a written answer with the clerk who issued this citation by 10:00 a.m. on the Monday next following the expiration of twenty days after you were served this citation and petition, a default judgment may be taken against you.

TO: _____ Defendant, Greeting:

You are hereby commanded to appear by filing a written answer to the Plaintiff's Petition at or before ten o'clock a.m. of the Monday next after the expiration of twenty days after the date of service of this citation before the ____ District Court of _____ County, Texas, at the courthouse of said County in the City of _____, Texas.

Said Plaintiff's Petition was filed in said court on the ____ day of _____, 20___, in this case, numbered _____, and styled

_____, Petitioner, and _____, Respondent.

The nature of Petitioner's demand is fully shown by a true and correct copy of the Petition accompanying this citation and made a part hereof.

The officer executing this writ shall promptly serve the same according to requirements of law, and the mandates thereof, and make due return as the law directs. Issued and given under my hand and seal of said Court at _____, Texas, this ____ day of _____, 20___,

Attest: _____

Clerk, District Court, _____ County, Texas

By _____, Deputy.

RETURN

The State of _____
County of _____

Before me, the undersigned authority, on this day personally appeared _____ _____, a person not interested in the within-mentioned suit, above 21 years of age, of sound mind and competent to make oath, and being sworn, deposed and said:

My name is _____; I am disinterested in the within styled and numbered cause, above 21 years of age, of sound mind and competent to make oath of the facts below:

The within citation came to hand on the _____ day of _____, 20___, at _____ o'clock (am)(pm), and was by me executed at _____ within the county of _____,at _____ o'clock (am)(pm), on the ____ day of _____, 20___, by delivering to the within named _____ in person, a true copy of this citation, having first endorsed thereon the date of delivery, together with the accompanying true and correct copy of the Petition.

The distance actually travelled by me in serving such process was ____ miles, and my fees are as follows:

For serving this citation......	$ _____
For mileage	$ _____
For notary	$ _____
Total fees	$ _____

Sheriff Account

No. _____

To certify which witness my hand officially: _____

Signed and sworn to by the said _____, before me this _____ day of _____, 20___, to certify which witness my hand and seal of office.

For Clerk's Use
Taxed _____
Return recorded _____

Notary Public, _____ County,

_____. (or other competent officer.)

INFORMATION FOR SERVICE OF PROCESS

FROM:_____

      Address: _____

      _____

      Phone(s): _____

TO: _____

      _____

      _____

    RE: In the Matter of the Marriage of:

         _____, Petitioner,

        and _____, Respondent.

        Cause No. _____

        In the _____ District Court of

        _____County, Texas

Dear Sir:

Enclosed are copies of a Petition and Citation, and a money order for $_____.

The enclosed papers **must** be served within 90 days of the date of issuance of the Citation in order to be valid. The Return portion of the Citation must, of course, be completely and accurately filled out and signed.

Note To Officers Outside The State Of Texas

The signature of the officer delivering the Citation and Petition MUST be sworn and Notarized in order to be effective in Texas.

Information For Service Of Process

Person to Be Served: _____

Residence Address: _____

_____

Work Address: _____

Other: _____

Physical Description: _____

_____

Comments:

Cause Number _____

IN THE MATTER OF THE MARRIAGE OF: IN THE DISTRICT COURT

_____, Petitioner

AND   ____ JUDICIAL DISTRICT

_____, Respondent   _____ COUNTY, TEXAS

AND IN THE INTEREST OF _____

_____ MINOR CHILD(REN)

FINAL DECREE OF DIVORCE

On the ___ day of _____, 20___, final hearing was held in this cause.

Petitioner, _____, who is the ☐ husband, ☐ wife, appeared in person, pro se, and announced ready for trial.

Respondent, _____

☐ personally appeared.
☐ has agreed to the terms of this Decree.
☐ was duly and properly cited by personal service and failed to appear.
☐ waived issuance and service of citation by Waiver of Citation duly filed.

☐ A record of testimony was made.
☐ The making of a record of testimony was waived by the parties with consent of the Court.

Because a jury was not demanded by either party, the Court tried the cause.

The Court, after reviewing the pleadings and receiving evidence, finds that the pleadings are in due form; that all residence requirements and prerequisites of law have been legally satisfied; that this Court has personal jurisdiction of the parties and of the subject matter of this cause; and that the material allegations of the Petition are true.

1.   **Divorce**

THE COURT FINDS that Petitioner and Respondent were married, and that their marriage had become insupportable and without any reasonable expectation of reconciliation.

THE COURT ORDERS that the marriage of Petitioner and Respondent is dissolved and that they are hereby divorced.

2. Children of the Marriage

☐ THE COURT FINDS that there is no unmarried child of the marriage under eighteen years of age and none is expected and that there are no children of the marriage over 18 who are disabled.

☐ THE COURT FINDS that Petitioner and Respondent are the parents of the following children:

Name:_____ Sex:___ Age:____ Birth date: _____
Present residence: _____
Birthplace: _____ Home State: _____

Name:_____ Sex:___ Age:____ Birth date: _____
Present residence: _____
Birthplace: _____ Home State: _____

Name:_____ Sex:___ Age:____ Birth date: _____
Present residence: _____
Birthplace: _____ Home State: _____

Name:_____ Sex:___ Age:____ Birth date: _____
Present residence: _____
Birthplace: _____ Home State: _____

Name:_____ Sex:___ Age:____ Birth date: _____
Present residence: _____
Birthplace: _____ Home State: _____

THE COURT FINDS that there are no other children of the marriage under age 18 or otherwise entitled to support and that none are expected.

THE COURT FINDS that the children do not own or possess any property other than their personal effects ☐ except as stated in Exhibit ___.

☐ The husband is **NOT** the biological father of the following children born during the marriage and that no legal relationship exists between these children and the husband:

Name:_____ Sex:___ Age:____ Birth date: _____

Name:_____ Sex:___ Age:____ Birth date: _____

Name:_____ Sex:___ Age:____ Birth date: _____

3. Conservatorship (custody)

THE COURT ORDERS that conservatorship, rights, duties, and responsibilities are awarded as provided in Exhibit ___, which is attached and incorporated into this Decree for all purposes.

4. Possession Schedule

THE COURT ORDERS that the parties shall have possession of the child(ren) as set forth in Exhibit ___, which is incorporated into this Decree for all purposes.

In this Decree, ☐ Petitioner ☐ Respondent is the Home Parent and the other party is the Co-Parent.

☐ For any child now under three years of age, the above schedule shall take effect on the child's third birthday. Until such time, the schedule shall be at times and places set forth in the attached Possession Order For Children Under Three Years, Exhibit ___, which is incorporated into this Decree for all purposes.

5. Child Support

THE COURT ORDERS that child support shall be paid as set forth in Exhibit ___, which is attached and incorporated into this Decree for all purposes.

6. Health Insurance

THE COURT ORDERS that health insurance shall be provided as set forth in Exhibit ___, which is attached and incorporated into this Decree for all purposes.

7. Warnings to parties and Notices to Others Regarding Child Support and Possession

Each person who is a party to this order is ordered to notify each other party, the court, and the state case registry of any change in the party's current residence address, mailing address, home telephone number, name of employer, address of employment, driver's license number, and work telephone number. The party is ordered to give notice of an intended change in any of the required information to each other party, the court, and the state case registry on or before the 60th day before the intended change. If the party does not know or could not have known of the change in sufficient time to provide 60-day notice, the party is ordered to give notice of the change on or before the fifth day after the date that the party knows of the change.

The duty to furnish this information to each other party, the court, and the state case registry continues as long as any person, by virtue of this order, is under an obligation to pay child support or entitled to possession of or access to a child.

Failure by a party to obey the order of this court to provide each other party, the court, and the state case registry with the change in the required information may result in further litigation to enforce the order, including contempt of court. A finding of contempt may be punished by confinement in jail for up to six months, a fine of up to $500 for each violation, and a money judgment for payment of attorney's fees and court costs.

Notice shall be given to the other party by delivering a copy of the notice to the party by registered or certified mail, return receipt requested. Notice shall be given to the court and the state case registry by delivering a copy of the notice either in person to the clerk of the Court or by registered or certified mail addressed to the clerk.

☐ **Petitioner** ☐ **Respondent is not required to furnish the above information.**

Failure to obey a court order for child support or for possession of or access to a child may result in further litigation to enforce the order, including contempt of court. A finding of contempt may be punished by confinement in jail for up to six months, a fine of up to $500 for each violation, and a money judgment for payment of attorney's fees and court costs.

Failure of a party to make a child support payment to the place and in the manner required by a court order may result in the party's not receiving credit for the payment.

Failure of a party to pay child support does not justify denying that party court-ordered possession of or access to a child. Refusal by a party to allow possession of or access to a child does not justify failure to pay court-ordered child support to that party.

IT IS ORDERED that each parent shall have the duty to inform the other parent if the parent resides with for at least 30 days, marries, or intends to marry a person who the parent knows: 1) is registered as a sex offender under chapter 62, code of criminal procedure; or 2) is currently charged with an offense for which on conviction the person would be required to register under that chapter. This notice shall be made as soon as practicable but not later than the 40th day after the date the parent begins to reside with the person or the 10th day after the date the marriage occurs, as appropriate. The notice must include a description of the offense that is the basis of the person's requirement to register as a sex offender or of the offense with which the person is charged.

A parent commits a Class C misdemeanor offense if he or she fails to provide notice in the manner ordered.

8. **Information Regarding Parties And Children**
   Required by Section 105.006 of the Texas Family Code

   ☐ The information required by § 105.006 of the Texas Family Code is attached in Exhibit ___, which is incorporated herein for all purposes.

   ☐ **Protection from identity theft.** The information required by § 105.006 of the Texas Family Code is attached in Exhibit ___, which is incorporated herein for all purposes. THE COURT FINDS that making personal information available to the public would expose the parties ☐ and their child(ren) to unnecessary risk of identity theft.

   THEREFORE IT IS ORDERED that ☐ this Exhibit ☐ the Decree and all attachments be sealed and made unavailable to the public.

   ☐ **Protection from abuse.** THE COURT FINDS, pursuant to Texas Family Code section 105.006(c), requiring ☐ Petitioner ☐ Respondent to provide the information required by section 105.006 is likely to cause the party or a child harassment, abuse, serious harm or injury. Accordingly, IT IS ORDERED that ☐ Petitioner ☐ Respondent is not required to provide the information required by Texas Family Code section 105.006.

9. Separate and Community Property and Debts

☐ THE COURT FINDS THAT the parties do not own any separate or community property of any significant value other than their personal effects. IT IS ORDERED that each party is awarded the personal effects presently in his/her possession as his/her separate property.

☐ THE COURT FINDS THAT the parties have entered into a written agreement for the division of their property and debts and that the agreement is just and right. IT IS ORDERED that the agreement of the parties, which is attached hereto and incorporated herein for all purposes, be and is approved.

☐ THE COURT FINDS THAT the parties possess separate and/or community property and debts which should be justly confirmed and/or divided. IT IS ORDERED that the estate of the parties is divided as set forth in Exhibit ___, which is attached and incorporated into this Decree for all purposes.

10. Income Taxes

THE COURT ORDERS that Petitioner and Respondent shall each be responsible for all taxes attributable to their own income only and each entitled to their own refunds for the year of the divorce.

☐ IT IS FURTHER ORDERED that Petitioner shall pay ___ percent and Respondent shall pay ___ percent of any income tax liability accrued prior to the year of the divorce, and that Petitioner shall receive ___ percent and Respondent shall receive ___ percent of any income tax refund accrued prior to the year of the divorce.

11. Spousal Maintenance

☐ The Court finds maintenance should be awarded on the following grounds:

    ☐ Petitioner and Respondent were married at least ten (10) years.

    ☐ Respondent was convicted of or received deferred adjudication for a family violence crime within two years from the date of the filing of this Petition.

In addition to the above, Petitioner lacks sufficient property, including property distributed after this divorce, to provide for Petitioner's minimum reasonable needs; and Petitioner

    ☐ clearly lacks the earning ability in the labor market adequate to provide for Petitioner's minimum reasonable needs.

    ☐ is unable to support him/herself through employment because of an incapacitating physical or mental disability.

    ☐ is the custodian of a child of this marriage who requires substantial care and personal supervision because of a physical or mental disability which makes it necessary that Petitioner not be employed outside of the home.

THEREFORE, THE COURT ORDERS that ☐ Petitioner ☐ Respondent pay to
☐ Petitioner ☐ Respondent for spousal maintenance the sum of $_____ per month, due and
payable beginning _____, 20___ and continuing on the same day of each month
thereafter until either party dies; or the receiving party remarries. This order for maintenance shall
continue for ____ months or further order of this court. All payments shall be made to any address
designated in writing by the recipient.

12. Mediation

THE COURT ORDERS, and the Parties agree, that in the event disputes arise between the parties,
the parties will seek mediation to resolve the disputes before any judicial proceeding, unless the
matter to be determined concerns a serious question regarding the health and safety of the child.

13. Name Change
☐ IT IS ORDERED AND DECREED THAT the name of _____
is hereby changed back to _____.

Signed and entered this ____ day of _____, 20___.

_____
Judge Presiding

Exhibits Attached:
☐ Exhibit __   Property Owned by Children
☐ Exhibit __   Conservatorship
☐ Exhibit __   Standard Possession Order
☐ Exhibit __   Possession Order for Children Under Three Years
☐ Exhibit __   Child Support Order
☐ Exhibit __   Health Insurance for Children
☐ Exhibit __   Information Required by Texas Family Code § 105.006
☐ Exhibit __   Orders re Property and Debts

I approve and consent as to both form and substance:

Date: _____   Date: _____

_____   _____
Petitioner   Respondent

Cause Number _____

Exhibit ___. Property Owned by Children of the Parties

THE COURT FINDS that the parties' child(ren) is/are possessed of the following property in addition to personal effects.

Name of child: _____

<u>Item</u>   <u>Value</u>

Name of child: _____

<u>Item</u>   <u>Value</u>

Name of child: _____

<u>Item</u>   <u>Value</u>

Cause Number _____

Exhibit _____. **Conservatorship Order**

The Court, having considered the circumstances of the parents and of the children, finds that the following orders are in the best interest of the children:

☐ Joint Managing Conservators. IT IS ORDERED that Petitioner and Respondent are appointed Joint Managing Conservators of the children subject of this cause.

☐ Sole Managing and Possessory Conservators. IT IS ORDERED that:

    ☐ Petitioner ☐ Respondent is appointed Sole Managing Conservator, and

    ☐ Petitioner ☐ Respondent is appointed Possessory Conservator

of the children subject of this cause.

The Home Parent is   ☐ Petitioner ☐ Respondent

The Co-Parent is   ☐ Petitioner ☐ Respondent

A. Exclusive Rights of the Home-Parent

1. The Home Parent has the exclusive right to designate the primary residence of the children

    ☐ anywhere, without any geographic restrictions.

    ☐ in this county.

    ☐ in this county or an adjacent county.

    ☐ in Texas.

    ☐ within the following geographic area (e.g. city, county, state, school district):

2. The Home Parent has the exclusive right to receive and give receipt for child support payments, and to save or use these funds for the children's benefit.

B. Parent's Rights and Duties During His or Her Periods of Possession

IT IS ORDERED that, during their respective periods of possession, Petitioner and Respondent, as conservators, shall have the following rights and duties:

1. The duty of care, control, protection, and reasonable discipline of the children;

2. The duty to support the children, including providing the children with food, clothing, shelter, and medical, and dental care not involving an invasive procedure;

3. The right to consent for the children to receive medical and dental care not involving an invasive procedure; and

4. The right to direct the moral and religious training of the children.

C. Parents' Rights and Duties at All Times

IT IS ORDERED that, at all times, Petitioner and Respondent, as conservators of the children, shall each have the following rights and duties:

1. The right to receive information from any other conservator of the children concerning the health, education, and welfare of the children;

2. The duty to inform any other conservator in a timely manner of significant information concerning the health, education, and welfare of the children;

3. The right to confer with any other conservator to the extent possible before making a decision concerning the health, education, and welfare of the children;

4. The right of access to medical, dental, psychological, and educational records of the children;

5. The right to consult with physicians, dentists, or psychologists of the children;

6. The right to consult with school officials concerning the children's welfare and educational status, including school activities;

7. The right to attend school activities;

8. The right to be designated on the children's records as a person to be notified in case of an emergency;

9. The right to consent to medical, dental, and surgical treatment during an emergency involving an immediate danger to the health and safety of the children; and

10. The right to manage the estates of the children to the extent the estates have been created by the parent or the parent's family.

D. Other Rights and Duties

IT IS ORDERED that Petitioner and Respondent, as parent conservators, shall share the following rights and duties in the manner indicated:

	Petitioner makes all decisions.	Respondent makes all decisions.	Parents make decisions together.	Each parent can make decisions without talking to the other parent about it.
The right to consent to medical, dental, and surgical treatment involving invasive procedures and to consent to psychological treatment of the children;	☐	☐	☐	☐
The right to represent the children in legal action and to make other decisions of substantial legal significance concerning the children;	☐	☐	☐	☐
The right to consent to marriage and to enlistment in the armed forces of the United States;	☐	☐	☐	☐
The right to make decisions concerning the children's education;	☐	☐	☐	☐
The right to services and earnings of the children;	☐	☐	☐	☐
Except when a guardian of the children's estates or a guardian or attorney ad litem has been appointed for the children, the right to act as an agent of the children in relation to the children's estates if the children's action is required by a state, the United States, or a foreign government; and	☐	☐	☐	☐
The duty to manage the estates of the children to the extent the estates have been created by community property or the joint property of the parents.	☐	☐	☐	☐

Exhibit ___. Standard Possession Order

_____ is the Home Parent and

_____ is the Co-Parent.

IT IS ORDERED that the conservators (Home Parent and Co-Parent) shall have possession of the child at times mutually agreed to in advance, but in the absence of agreement they shall have possession of the child under the terms ORDERED below.

Parental Rights and Duties. Home Parent shall have the right to decide where the child's home will be, as specified more particularly in the Conservatorship Order, where all parental rights and duties are defined.

I. PARENTS WHO RESIDE 100 MILES OR LESS APART

a. **Co-Parent Possession.** Unless this Possession Order says differently, when Co-Parent resides 100 miles or less from the primary residence of the child, **Co-Parent** shall have the right to possession of the child as follows:

1. **Weekends**. On the first, third, and fifth Friday of each month. This possession begins and ends at the times specified in the General Terms and Conditions of this Possession Order.

2. **Thursdays**. On Thursday of each week during the regular school term. This possession begins and ends at the times specified in the General Terms and Conditions of this Possession Order.

3. **Spring Break in Even-Numbered Years**. In even-numbered years, this possession begins and ends at the times specified in the General Terms and Conditions of this Possession Order.

4. **Extended Summer Possession by Co-Parent**

   A. **With Written Notice by April 1**. If Co-Parent gives Home Parent written notice by April 1 of a year specifying an extended period or periods of summer possession for that year, Co-Parent shall have possession of the child for thirty days beginning no earlier than the day after the child's school is dismissed for the summer vacation and ending no later than seven days before school resumes at the end of the summer vacation in that year, to be exercised in no more than two separate periods of at least seven consecutive days each, as specified in the written notice. These periods of possession shall begin and end at 6:00 p.m. on the first and last days of each period.

   B. **Without Written Notice by April 1**. If Co-Parent does **not** give Home Parent written notice by April 1 of a year specifying an extended period or periods of summer possession for that year, Co-Parent shall have possession of the child for thirty consecutive days in that year beginning at 6:00 p.m. on July 1 and ending at 6:00 p.m. on July 31.

b. **Home Parent Possession.** Notwithstanding the weekend periods of possession ORDERED for Co-Parent, it is explicitly ORDERED that Home Parent shall have a superior right of possession of the child as follows:

1. **Spring Break in Odd-Numbered Years.** In odd-numbered years, beginning on the day the child is dismissed from school for spring vacation at (choose one): ☐ 6:00 p.m. ☐ the time the child is regularly dismissed from school and ending at 6:00 p.m. on the day before school resumes after that vacation.

2. **Summer Weekend Possession by Home Parent.** If Home Parent gives Co-Parent written notice by April 15 of a year, Home Parent shall have possession of the child on any one weekend beginning at 6:00 p.m. on Friday and ending at 6:00 p.m. on the following Sunday during any one period of the extended summer possession by Co-Parent in that year, provided that Home Parent picks up the child from Co-Parent and returns the child to that same place.

3. **Extended Summer Possession by Home Parent.** If Home Parent gives Co-Parent written notice by April 1 of a year or gives Co-Parent fourteen days' written notice on or after April 1 of a year, Home Parent may designate one weekend beginning no earlier than the day after the child's school is dismissed for the summer vacation and ending no later than seven days before school resumes at the end of the summer vacation, during which an otherwise scheduled weekend period of possession by Co-Parent shall not take place in that year, provided that the weekend so designated does not interfere with Co-Parent's period or periods of extended summer possession or with Father's Day if father is Home-Parent.

Home Parent shall have the right of possession of the child at all other times not specifically designated in this Possession Order for *Co-Parent*.

[This concludes weekly, spring break, and summer visitation for parents who live less than 100 miles apart. See also Holiday Visitation and General Terms and Conditions.]

II. PARENTS WHO RESIDE MORE THAN 100 MILES APART

a. **Co-Parent Possession when Parents Reside More Than 100 Miles Apart.** Unless this Possession Order states differently, when Co-Parent resides more than 100 miles from the residence of the child, **Co-Parent** shall have the right to possession of the child as follows:

1. **Weekends.** Unless Co-Parent elects the alternative period of weekend possession described in the next paragraph, Co-Parent shall have the right to possession of the child on the first, third, and fifth Friday of each month. This possession begins and ends at the times specified in the General Terms and Conditions of this Possession Order.

2. **Alternate Weekend Possession.** In lieu of the weekend possession described in the above paragraph, Co-Parent shall have the right to possession of the child not

more than one weekend per month of Co-Parent's choice. This possession begins and ends at the times specified in the General Terms and Conditions of this Possession Order.

Co-Parent may choose this alternative period of weekend possession by giving written notice to Home Parent within ninety days after the parties begin to reside more than 100 miles apart. If Co-Parent chooses this Alternative Weekend Possession, Co-Parent shall give Home Parent fourteen days' written or telephonic notice of the chosen weekend. Co-Parent cannot choose a weekend that interferes with the orders regarding Christmas, Thanksgiving, the child's birthday, and Father's or Mother's Day Weekend.

3. **Spring Break in All Years.** Every year, beginning and ending at the times specified in the General Terms and Conditions of this Possession Order.

4. **Extended Summer Possession by Co-Parent**
   A. **With Written Notice by April 1.** If Co-Parent gives Home Parent written notice by April 1 of a year specifying an extended period or periods of summer possession for that year, Co-Parent shall have possession of the child for forty-two days beginning no earlier than the day after the child's school is dismissed for the summer vacation and ending no later than seven days before school resumes at the end of the summer vacation in that year, to be exercised in no more than two separate periods of at least seven consecutive days each, as specified in the written notice. These periods of possession shall begin and end at 6:00 p.m. on the first and last days of each period.

   B. **Without Written Notice by April 1.** If Co-Parent does not give Home Parent written notice by April 1 of a year specifying an extended period or periods of summer possession for that year, Co-Parent shall have possession of the child for forty-two consecutive days beginning at 6:00 p.m. on June 15 and ending at 6:00 p.m. on July 27 of that year.

b. **Home Parent Possession when Parents Reside More Than 100 Miles Apart.** Notwithstanding the weekend periods of possession ORDERED for Co-Parent, it is explicitly ORDERED that *Home Parent* shall have a superior right of possession of the child as follows:

1. **Summer Weekend Possession by Home Parent.** If Home Parent gives Co-Parent written notice by April 15 of a year, Home Parent shall have possession of the child on any one weekend beginning at 6:00 p.m. on Friday and ending at 6:00 p.m. on the following Sunday during any one period of possession by Co-Parent during Co-Parent's extended summer possession in that year, provided that if a period of possession by Co-Parent in that year exceeds thirty days, Home Parent may have possession of the child under the terms of this provision on any two nonconsecutive weekends during that period and provided that Home Parent picks up the child from Co-Parent and returns the child to that same place.

2. **Extended Summer Possession by Home Parent.** If Home Parent gives Co-Parent written notice by April 15 of a year, Home Parent may designate twenty-

one days beginning no earlier than the day after the child's school is dismissed for the summer vacation and ending no later than seven days before school resumes at the end of the summer vacation in that year, to be exercised in no more than two separate periods of at least seven consecutive days each, with each period of possession beginning and ending at 6 p.m. on the first and last days of each period, during which Co-Parent shall not have possession of the child, provided that the period or periods so designated do not interfere with Co-Parent's period or periods of extended summer possession or with Father's Day if the father is Co-Parent.

Home Parent shall have the right of possession of the child at all other times not specifically designated in this Possession Order for **Co-Parent**.

[This concludes weekly, spring break, and summer visitation for parents who live more than 100 miles from each other. See also Holiday Visitation and General Terms and Conditions.]

III. HOLIDAY VISITATION

These orders regarding holiday visitation override conflicting weekend or Thursday visitation orders, no matter the distance between parents' residences.

a. **Co-Parent shall have right of possession of the child during holiday visitation as follows:**

1. **Christmas Holidays in Even-Numbered Years**
    In even-numbered years, beginning at the time provided for in the General Terms and Conditions of this Possession Order, and ending at noon on December 26.

2. **Christmas Holidays in Odd-Numbered Years**
    In odd-numbered years, beginning at noon on December 26, and ending at the time provided for in the General Terms and Conditions of this Possession Order.

3. **Thanksgiving in Odd-Numbered Years**
    In odd-numbered years, this possession begins and ends at the times provided for in the General Terms and Conditions of this Possession Order.

4. **Child's Birthday** [Check box if appropriate]
    If Co-Parent is not otherwise entitled under this Possession Order to possession of the child on the child's birthday, Co-Parent shall have possession of the child, ☐ and the child's siblings, beginning at 6:00 p.m. and ending at 8:00 p.m. on that day, provided that Co-Parent picks up the child from Home Parent's residence and returns the child to that same place.

5. **Parent's Weekend** [check only the Parent's Day that applies to the visiting Co-Parent]
    ☐ Father's Day Weekend. Each year, beginning at 6:00 p.m. on the Friday before Father's Day and ending at ☐ 6:00 p.m. on Father's Day ☐ 8 a.m. on the Monday after Father's Day weekend, provided that if he is not otherwise entitled under this Possession Order to possession of the child, he shall pick up and return the child at Home Parent's residence.

☐ Mother's Day Weekend. Each year, beginning at
    ☐ 6:00 p.m. on the Friday before Mother's Day
    ☐ the time the child's school is regularly dismissed on the Friday preceding
Mother's Day, and ending at
    ☐ 6:00 p.m. on Mother's Day
    ☐ 8 a.m. on the Monday after Mother's Day weekend,
provided that if she is not otherwise entitled under this Possession Order to
possession of the child, she shall pick up and return the child at Home Parent's
residence.

b. Notwithstanding the weekend and Thursday periods of possession ORDERED for
Co-Parent, it is explicitly ORDERED that ***Home Parent*** shall have a superior right of
possession of the child during holidays as follows:

1. **Christmas Holidays in Odd-Numbered Years**
   In odd-numbered years, beginning at 6:00 p.m. on the day the child is dismissed
   from school for Christmas school vacation and ending at noon on December 26.

2. **Christmas Holidays in Even-Numbered Years**
   In even-numbered years, beginning at noon on December 26 and ending at 6 p.m.
   on the day before school resumes.

3. **Thanksgiving in Even-Numbered Years**
   In even-numbered years, beginning at 6:00 p.m. on the day the child is dismissed
   from school for the Thanksgiving holiday and ending at 6:00 p.m. on the
   following Sunday.

4. **Child's Birthday**   [Check box if appropriate]
   If Home Parent is not otherwise entitled under this Possession Order to possession
   of the child on the child's birthday, Home Parent shall have possession of the
   child, ☐ and the child's siblings, beginning at 6:00 p.m. and ending at 8:00 p.m.
   on that day, provided that Home Parent picks up the child from Co-Parent's
   residence and returns the child to that same place.

5. **Parent's Weekend**   [Check only one]
   ☐ Father's Day Weekend. Each year, beginning at 6:00 p.m. on the Friday
   before Father's Day and ending at 6:00 p.m. on Father's Day, provided that if
   Home Parent is not otherwise entitled under this Possession Order to possession
   of the child, he shall pick up the child from Co-Parent's residence and return the
   child to that same place.

   ☐ Mother's Day Weekend. Each year, beginning at 6:00 p.m. on the Friday
   before Mother's Day and ending at 6:00 p.m. on Mother's Day, provided that if
   Home Parent is not otherwise entitled under this Possession Order to possession
   of the child, she shall pick up the child from Co-Parent's residence and return the
   child to that same place.

[This concludes the Holiday Visitation. See also General Terms and Conditions.]

IV. GENERAL TERMS AND CONDITIONS

Except as otherwise explicitly provided in this Possession Order, the following terms and conditions of possession of the child that regardless of the distance between the residence of a parent and the child:

Home Parent shall have the right of possession of the child at all other times not specifically designated in this Possession Order for **Co-Parent**.

"School" means the primary or secondary school in which the child is enrolled or, if the child is not enrolled in a primary or secondary school, the public school district in which the child primarily resides.

"Child" includes each child, whether one or more, who is a subject of this suit while that child is under the age of eighteen years and not otherwise emancipated.

a. Surrendering and Returning of Child by Home Parent

1. **Beginning of Co-Parent's Weekend, Thursday, and Holiday Possession.** Home Parent is ORDERED to surrender the child to Co-Parent at the beginning of each period of Co-Parent's possession at: [Check only one]

    ☐ 6:00 p.m.
    ☐ The time the child is regularly dismissed from school before the visitation

    Except, that in odd-numbered years, Co-Parent's Christmas possession begins at noon on December 26, and Home Parent is ORDERED to surrender the child to Co-Parent at this time.

2. **Co-Parent picks up the child from Home Parent's residence, unless a period of possession begins at the time the child is regularly dismissed from school.** Home Parent is ORDERED to surrender the child to Co-Parent at the beginning of each period of Co-Parent's possession at the residence of Home Parent.

3. **Co-Parent picks up the child from school, if a period of possession begins at the time the child's school is regularly dismissed.** If a period of possession by Co-Parent begins at the time the child's school is regularly dismissed, Home Parent is ORDERED to surrender the child to Co-Parent at the beginning of each such period of possession at the school in which the child is enrolled.

4. If the child is not in school, Co-Parent shall pick up the child at the residence of Home Parent at:

    ☐ 6:00 p.m. ☐ _____ [Insert time and specify a.m. or p.m.]

    and Home Parent is ORDERED to surrender the child to Co-Parent at the residence of Home Parent at this time under these circumstances.

b. Surrendering and Returning the Child by Co-Parent

1. **Ending of Co-Parent's Weekend & Holiday Possession**
   Co-Parent is ORDERED to surrender the child to Home Parent at: [Check only one]
   ☐ 6:00 p.m. on the Sunday following the visitation
   ☐ The time the child's school resumes after the visitation.

   Except that in even-numbered years, Co-Parent's Christmas possession ends at noon on December 26, and Co-Parent is ORDERED to surrender the child to Home Parent at this time.

2. **Ending of Co-Parent's Thursday Possession**
   Co-Parent is ORDERED to surrender the child to Home Parent at: [Check only one]
   ☐ 8:00 p.m.   ☐ The time the child's school resumes on Friday.

3. **Weekend Possession Extended by a Holiday**
   Unless this Possession Order says differently:

   (a) If a weekend period of possession by Co-Parent begins on a Friday that
       (i) during the regular school term, as determined by the school in which the child is enrolled, is a student holiday or teacher in-service day, or
       (ii) during summer months when school is not in session, is a federal, state, or local holiday,
   then the weekend period of possession shall BEGIN at: [Check only one]
       ☐ 6:00 p.m. on the Thursday preceding the Friday holiday;
       ☐ The time the child's school is regularly dismissed on the Thursday immediately preceding the Friday holiday;

   (b) If a weekend period of possession by Co-Parent ends on or is immediately followed by a Monday that
       (i) during the regular school term, as determined by the school in which the child is enrolled, is a student holiday or teacher in-service day, or
       (ii) during summer months when school is not in session, is a federal, state, or local holiday,
   then the weekend period of possession shall END at: [Check only one]
       ☐ 6:00 p.m. on that Monday holiday.
       ☐ The time school next resumes after that holiday.

4. **Place of surrender and return of child by Co-Parent**   [Check only one]
   ☐ Surrender of Child by Co-Parent. Co-Parent is ORDERED to surrender the child to Home Parent at the residence of Co-Parent at the end of each period of possession.

   ☐ Return of Child by Co-Parent. Co-Parent is ORDERED to return the child to the residence of Home Parent at the end of each period of possession. However, it is ORDERED that, if Home Parent and Co-Parent live in the same county at the time of rendition of this order, and Co-Parent's county of residence remains the same after rendition of this order, and Home Parent's county of residence changes, effective on the date of the change of residence by Home Parent, Co-

Parent shall surrender the child to Home Parent at the residence of Co-Parent at the end of each period of possession.

5. **Co-Parent returns the child to school if a period of possession by Co-Parent ends at the *time the child's school resumes*.** If a period of possession by Co-Parent ends at the time the child's school resumes, Co-Parent is ORDERED to deliver the child to Home Parent at the end of each period of possession at the school in which the child is enrolled, but if the child is not in school, Co-Parent returns the child to the residence of Home Parent at: [Check one]
☐ 8:00 a.m. ☐ _____ [Insert time, specify a.m. or p.m.]

c. Personal Effects of Child
Each party is ORDERED to return with the child the personal effects that the child brought at the beginning of the period of possession.

d. Designation of Competent Adult
Each party may designate any competent adult to pick up and return the child, as applicable. IT IS ORDERED that a party or a designated competent adult be present when the child is picked up or returned.

e. Inability to Exercise Possession
Each party is ORDERED to give notice to the person in possession of the child on each occasion that the party will be unable to exercise that party's right of possession for any specified period.

f. Written Notice
Written notice shall be deemed to have been timely made if received or postmarked on or before the time that notice is due.

g. Notice to School and Home Parent
If Co-Parent's time of possession of the child ends at the time school resumes and for any reason the child is not or will not be returned to school, Co-Parent shall immediately notify the school and Home Parent that the child will not be or has not been returned to school.

h. Notice to any Peace Officer of the State of Texas
YOU MAY USE REASONABLE EFFORTS TO ENFORCE THE TERMS OF CHILD CUSTODY SPECIFIED IN THIS ORDER. A PEACE OFFICER WHO RELIES ON THE TERMS OF A COURT ORDER, AND HIS AGENCY, ARE ENTITLED TO THE APPLICABLE IMMUNITY AGAINST ANY CLAIM, CIVIL OR OTHERWISE, REGARDING THE OFFICER'S GOOD FAITH ACTS PERFORMED IN THE SCOPE OF THE OFFICER'S DUTIES IN ENFORCING THE TERMS OF THE ORDER THAT RELATE TO CHILD CUSTODY.
Any person who knowingly presents for enforcement an order that is invalid or is no longer in effect commits an offense that may be punishable by confinement in jail for as long as two years and a fine of as much as $10,000.

Cause Number _____

Exhibit ___. Child Support Order

Obligor. In this order and this Exhibit: [Check one box on each line.]

☐ Petitioner ☐ Respondent is the Obligor, the person who must pay child support.

☐ Petitioner ☐ Respondent is the Obligee, the person who has a right to receive child support.

☐ **Section A. Constant Child Support Order**

IT IS ORDERED that Obligor must pay and shall pay child support to Obligee in the amount of $_____ per month. The first payment is due and payable on the first day of the first month immediately following the date this decree is signed.

IT IS FURTHER ORDERED that the same amount is due and payable on the first day of each month thereafter until the first month following the date on which one of the following events has occurred with respect to each and every subject child:

1. The child reaches the age of eighteen years, *provided that,*
   (a) The child is enrolled in an accredited secondary school program leading toward a high school diploma, or in courses for joint high school and junior college credit, or on a full-time basis in a private secondary school program leading toward a high school diploma; *and*
   (b) The child is complying with the minimum attendance requirements of Chapter 25 of the Education Code, or the minimum attendance requirements imposed by the school in which the child is enrolled, if the child is enrolled in a private secondary school;
   Then the periodic child-support payments shall continue to be due and paid until the end of the month in which the child graduates; or

2. The child marries; or

3. The child dies; or

4. The child's disabilities are otherwise removed for general purposes; or

5. The date on which the Court enters a further order modifying child support; or

6. The Court makes a finding that the child is 18 years of age or older and has failed to comply with the enrollment or attendance requirements described above; or

7. The marriage or re-marriage of Obligor and Obligee to each other.

☐ Section B. "Step Down Child Support Order"

IT IS ORDERED that Obligor must pay and shall pay child support to Obligee in the amount of $_____ per month. The first payment is due and payable on the first day of the first month immediately following the date this decree is signed.

IT IS FURTHER ORDERED that the same amount is due and payable on the first day of each month thereafter until the first month following the date on which one of the following events has occurred with respect to *any* child subject of this suit:
1. Any child reaches the age of eighteen years, *provided that,*
    (a) Any child is enrolled in an accredited secondary school program leading toward a high school diploma, or in courses for joint high school and junior college credit, or on a full-time basis in a private secondary school program leading toward a high school diploma; *and*
    (b) Any child is complying with the minimum attendance requirement*s* of Chapter 25 of the Education Code, or the minimum attendance requirements imposed by the school in which the child is enrolled, if the child is enrolled in a private secondary school;

    Then the periodic child-support payments shall continue to be due and paid until the end of the month in which the child graduates; or

2. Any child marries; or

3. Any child dies; or

4. Any child's disabilities are otherwise removed for general purposes; or

5. The date on which the Court enters a further order modifying child support; or

6. The Court makes a finding that the child is 18 years of age or older and has failed to comply with the enrollment or attendance requirements described above; or

7. The marriage or re-marriage of Obligor and Obligee to each other.

Thereafter, Obligor is ORDERED to pay to Obligee child support of $_____ per month, due and payable on the first day of the first month immediately following the date of the earliest occurrence of one of the events specified above for another child and the same amount being due on the first day of each month thereafter until the next occurrence of one of the events specified above for another child.

Thereafter, Obligor is ORDERED to pay to Obligee child support of $_____ per month, due and payable on the first day of the first month immediately following the date of the earliest occurrence of one of the events specified above for another child and the same amount being due on the first day of each month thereafter until the next occurrence of one of the events specified above for another child.

Thereafter, Obligor is ORDERED to pay to Obligee child support of $_____ per month, due and payable on the first day of the first month immediately following the date of the earliest occurrence of one of the events specified above for another child and the same amount being due on the first day of each month thereafter until the next occurrence of one of the events specified above for another child.

Thereafter, Obligor is ORDERED to pay to Obligee child support of $_____ per month, due and payable on the first day of the first month immediately following the date of the earliest occurrence of one of the events specified above for another child and the same amount being due on the first day of each month thereafter until the next occurrence of one of the events specified above for another child.

☐ **Section C. Deviation from Child Support Guidelines**

In accordance with Texas Family Code section 154.130, the Court makes the following findings and conclusions regarding the child-support order made in open court in this case on this day:

1. The application of the guidelines in this case would be unjust or inappropriate.

2. The net resources available to the Obligor (Co-Parent) per month is $_____.

3. The net resources available to the Obligee (Home Parent) per month is $_____.

4. The number of minor children before the Court is _____ (minor children husband and wife have together).

5. The names and birth dates of all children not before the Court who reside in the same household with the Obligor (Co-Parent) and/or for whom the Obligor (Co-Parent) has a legal duty to pay support are as follows:

    Full Name: _____ Birth Date: _____

    Full Name: _____ Birth Date: _____

    Full Name: _____ Birth Date: _____

    Full Name: _____ Birth Date: _____

    Full Name: _____ Birth Date: _____

    Full Name: _____ Birth Date: _____

6. If the percentage guidelines of section 154.125 or 154.129 of the Texas Family Code are applied to the first $6,000 of Obligor's (Co-Parent's) net resources, the amount of child-support payments per month is $_____.

7. The percentage applied to the first $6,000 of Obligor's (Co-Parent's) net resources for child support by the actual order rendered by the Court is _____ % (percent).

8. The specific reasons that the amount of child support per month ordered by the Court is different from the amount computed by applying the percentage guidelines of section 154.125 or 154.129 of the Texas Family Code are:

Section D. Withholding from Earnings

IT IS ORDERED that any employer of Obligor shall be ordered to withhold from earnings for child support from the disposable earnings of Obligor for the support of the children who are the subject of this suit.

☐ **Section E. Suspension of Withholding from Earnings**

The COURT FINDS that good cause exists, or the parties agree, that no order to withhold earnings for child support should be delivered to any employer of Obligor as long as no delinquency or other violation of the child-support order occurs. A delinquency occurs when Obligor is behind in child-support payments for more than thirty days, or the past due amount equals or is greater than the amount due for a one-month period. If a delinquency or other violation occurs, upon request, the clerk shall deliver the order to withhold earnings as provided in this order.

ACCORDINGLY, IT IS ORDERED that, as long as no delinquency or other violation of this child support order occurs, all payments shall be made through the Child Support State Disbursement Unit and then promptly forwarded to the Obligee for the support of the children. If a delinquency or other violation occurs, all payments shall be made according to the order to withhold earnings as provided in this order.

Section F. Withholding as Credit against Support Obligation

IT IS FURTHER ORDERED that all amounts withheld from the disposable earnings of Obligor by the employer and paid in accordance with the order to that employer shall constitute a credit against the child support obligation. Payment of the full amount of child support ordered paid by this decree through the means of withholding from earnings shall discharge the child-support obligation. If the amount withheld from earnings and credited against the child support obligation is less than 100 percent of the amount ordered to be paid by this decree, the balance due remains an obligation of Obligor, and it is hereby ORDERED that Obligor pay the balance due directly to the local registry of the court specified below.

Section G. Order to Employer

On this date the Court signed an Employer's Order to Withhold from Earnings for Child Support.

IT IS ORDERED that, on the request of a prosecuting attorney, the attorney general, Obligee, or Obligor, the clerk of this Court shall cause a certified copy of the "Employer's Order to Withhold from Earnings for Child Support" to be delivered to any employer.

IT IS FURTHER ORDERED that the clerk of this Court shall attach a copy of subchapter C of chapter 158 of the Texas Family Code for the information of any employer.

Section H. Payments through Child Support State Disbursement Unit.

IT IS ORDERED that all payments shall be made through Child Support State Disbursement Unit, PO Box 659791, San Antonio, Texas 78265-9791, and then forwarded by that agency to Obligee for support of the children.

☐ **Section I.** [Use this if your County has a Domestic Relations Office that requires this form]
Establishment of Account and Payment of Domestic Relations Office Service Fee

   (a) IT IS ORDERED THAT both the Obligor and Obligee shall complete a "Request to Establish an Account" form and deliver it to the Domestic Relations Office within five days after the court has approved and signed this decree.
   (b) Upon receipt of this form, the Domestic Relations Office shall set up and open an account in the State Disbursement Unit database in order that all payments of child support received by that Unit can be distributed according to law.
   (c) IT IS FURTHER ORDERED THAT, at the time an account is established at the Domestic Relations Office, that both the Obligor and Obligee shall each pay the required service fee, as authorized by Texas Family Code Section 203.005 (a)(5).
   (d) Each party is ordered to pay this fee each and every year that a child-support account remains active with the Domestic Relations Office.

Section J. No Credit for Informal Payments. IT IS ORDERED that the child support as prescribed in this decree shall be exclusively discharged in the manner ordered and that any direct payments made by Obligor to Obligee or any expenditures incurred by Obligor during Obligor's periods of possession of or access to the children, as prescribed in this decree, for food, clothing, gifts, travel, shelter, or entertainment are deemed in addition to and not in lieu of the support ordered in this decree.

Section K. Support as Obligation of Estate. IT IS ORDERED that the provisions for child support in this decree shall be an obligation of the estate of Obligor and shall not terminate on the death of Obligor. Payments received for the benefit of the children from the Social Security Administration, Department of Veteran's Affairs, other government agency, or life insurance shall be a credit against this obligation.

Section L. Notice of Change of Address. IT IS FURTHER ORDERED that Obligor shall notify this Court and Obligee by US certified mail, return receipt requested, of any changes of address and of any termination of employment. This notice shall be given no later than seven days after the change of address or the termination of employment. This notice or a subsequent notice shall also provide the current address of Obligor and the name and address of Obligor's current employer, whenever that information becomes available.

Cause Number _____

Exhibit ___. Health Insurance Order for Child(ren)

1. **Insurance Payor.** In this order and this Exhibit: [Check one]
   ☐ Petitioner ☐ Respondent is the Payor, the person who must provide and pay for health insurance for the children.

2. **Insurance Receiver.** In this order and this Exhibit [Check only one.]:
   ☐ Petitioner ☐ Respondent is the Insurance Receiver.

3. **Definitions**
   (a) "Health insurance" means insurance coverage that provides basic health-care services, including doctor services, office visits, hospitalization, laboratory, X-ray, and emergency services.
   (b) "Reasonable cost" means the cost of the health insurance premium is not more than 10% of the Payor's net monthly income.
   (c) "Through employment" means through the party's employment or membership in a union, trade association, or other organization.
   (d) "Insuring Party" means the person who actually provides the health insurance, either Payor or Receiver.
   (e) "Constructive trustee" means the person who is sent reimbursement from the insurance carrier.

4. **Payor's Responsibility.** Payor is ORDERED to provide health insurance for the children. Payor may provide health insurance through one of the following:
   (a) Payor's employment
   (b) Receiver's employment
   (c) Private health insurance
   (d) Public health insurance program
   (e) Monthly medical support payments

5. **Insurance through Payor's Employment.** If health insurance for the children is available through Payor's employment, at a reasonable cost, Payor IS ORDERED to insure the parties' children through Payor's employment.

6. **Insurance through Receiver's Employment**
   (a) If health insurance for the children is not available to Payor at a reasonable cost, but is available to Receiver at a reasonable cost, then Receiver IS ORDERED to cover the children as dependents on Receiver's health insurance plan, and Payor IS ORDERED to reimburse Receiver the cost of insuring the children.
   (b) Reimbursement is due on the first day of the first month following written request for payment, and on the first day of each month thereafter.

7. **If health insurance is not available at a reasonable cost**
   (a) If health insurance is not available at a reasonable cost for the children through <u>either</u> party's employment, Payor IS ORDERED to purchase health insurance for the party's children.

(b) Payor shall provide proof of coverage and the plan summary to Receiver within 7 days of obtaining coverage.

[Complete Section 8 only if, at the time of the divorce, Receiver provides health insurance, and Payor reimburses Receiver, **and** the reimbursement is already included in Payor's monthly child support.]

8. ☐ The Court finds that Receiver currently provides health insurance for the children at a cost of $_____ per month, and ORDERS that reimbursement for this monthly health insurance premium is included in Payor's monthly child-support amount of $_____.

The Court further ORDERS that this amount is due on the first day of the first month, after this order is signed, and on the first day of each month thereafter.

Should this health insurance no longer be available to Receiver, IT IS ORDERED that Payor shall provide health insurance for the children as described in this Exhibit.

9. **Conversion of Policy**
   (a) Should the Insuring Party lose insurance coverage for the children, the Insuring Party IS ORDERED to convert the policy to individual coverage for the children in an amount that equals or exceeds the coverage that was lost. This conversion must take place within ten days of losing coverage.
   (b) If Receiver converts the policy, Payor IS ORDERED to reimburse Receiver for the cost of the converted policy. Reimbursement is due on the first day of the first month following written request for payment, and on the first day of each month thereafter.

[Complete Section 10 only if the parties agree, or the Court finds that health insurance is not affordable.]

10. ☐ **Private Health Insurance Not Affordable**
   (a) If health insurance is not available to Payor at a reasonable cost through Payor's employment or Receiver's employment, and Payor is not financially able to provide insurance from another source, IT IS ORDERED that Payor shall obtain and maintain health coverage for the children through the TexCare Partnership, (800) 647-6558, www.texcarepartnership.com.
   (b) If health coverage for the children is not available through the TexCare Partnership, IT IS ORDERED that Payor shall pay the sum of $_____ per month to Receiver as medical support for the children, and that payment is included in Payor's monthly child-support amount of $_____. The Court further ORDERS that this amount is due and payable on the first day of the first month after this order is signed, and on the first day of each month thereafter.

11. **Claim Forms.** If the insurance company requires claim forms to be filed for reimbursement, then each party IS ORDERED to submit all forms, receipts, bills, and statements needed to complete the claim within ten days of receiving them.

12. **Constructive Trust for Payments Received.** IT IS ORDERED that any insurance payments received belong to the party who paid those expenses.

IT IS FURTHER ORDERED that a party who receives insurance payments is designated a constructive trustee for the party who paid the expenses. The constructive trustee shall endorse and forward the payments, along with any explanation of benefits, to the paying party within three days of receiving them.

13. **Filing by Party Not Carrying Insurance.** IT IS ORDERED that either party, even the Non-Insuring party, may file claims for health care expenses directly with the Insurance carrier.

IT IS FURTHER ORDERED that solely for purposes of article 3.51-13 of the Texas Insurance Code, the Non-Insuring Party is designated the managing conservator of the children.

14. **Secondary Coverage.** Either party may provide secondary health insurance coverage for the children at his or her sole cost and expense. Should secondary health insurance cover the children, IT IS ORDERED that both parties shall maximize the insurance benefits available to the children.

15. **Payment of Uninsured Expenses**
    (a) Each party IS ORDERED to pay one-half (50%) of all reasonable and necessary uninsured healthcare expenses of the parties' children (for example: annual deductible and prescription drug, dental, eye care, and orthodontic charges; expenses that are not covered by health insurance), for as long as child support is ordered under the terms of this decree.
    (b) Each party IS ORDERED to submit all receipts for uninsured health-care expenses for the children to the other party within ten days of receiving them.
    (c) IT IS FURTHER ORDERED that the non-paying party shall pay his or her half of the uninsured health-care expenses to the other party or the health-care provider within ten days of receiving the receipts.
    (d) Exclusions. The provisions above concerning uninsured expenses do not include expenses for travel to and from the health-care provider or nonprescription medication.

16. **Reasonableness of Charges.** IT IS ORDERED that all health care expenses are presumed reasonable. This presumption does not change even when a claim has been denied by a health insurer.

17. **Information Required**
    (a) IT IS ORDERED that the Insuring Party shall furnish to the other party the following information within 30 days from when this order is signed:
        (1) The Social Security number of the Insuring Party;
        (2) The name and address of the employer of the Insuring Party;
        (3) Whether the employer is self-insured or has health insurance available;
        (4) Proof that health insurance has been provided for the children; and
        (5) The name of the health insurance carrier, the number of the policy, a copy of the policy and schedule of benefits, a health insurance membership card, claim forms, and any other information necessary to submit a claim; or, if the

claim forms, and any other information necessary to submit a claim; or, if the employer is self-insured, a copy of the schedule of benefits, a membership card, claim forms, and any other information necessary to submit a claim.

(b) IT IS FURTHER ORDERED that the Insuring Party shall furnish to the other party a copy of any renewals or changes to the policy within 15 days of receiving them.

(c) Additionally, IT IS ORDERED that the Insuring Party shall provide to the other party any additional information regarding health insurance coverage that becomes available to him or her, within 15 days of receiving it.

18. **United States Code, Title 29, Section 1169.** For the purpose of Section 1169 of Title 29 of the United States Code, the party not carrying the health insurance policy is designated the custodial parent and alternate recipient's representative.

19. **Termination or Lapse of Insurance**. The Insuring Party IS ORDERED to notify the other party within 15 days of a termination or lapse in insurance coverage.

Payor must notify Receiver if additional health insurance becomes available within 15 days of its availability. Payor must enroll the children in a health insurance plan at the next available enrollment period.

20. **Place for Correspondence**. IT IS ORDERED that all correspondence required by the health care provision of this decree shall be sent to the receiving party's mailing address, as he or she has provided in compliance with this decree.

21. **WARNING.** A parent who fails to provide or pay for health insurance, as ordered, or who fails to pay the other parent additional child support for the cost of health insurance, as ordered, is liable for all reasonable and necessary medical expenses of the children, whether or not the expenses would have been paid if health insurance had been provided

Exhibit ___

INFORMATION REQUIRED BY TEXAS FAMILY CODE SECTION 105.006

The information that is required by section 105.006(a) of the Texas Family Code is as follows:

Name of Petitioner: _____
    Social Security number: _____
    Driver's license number: _____ Issuing state: _____
    Current residence address: _____
    Mailing address: _____
    Home telephone number: _____ Work phone: _____
    Name of employer: _____
    Address of employment: _____

Name of Respondent: _____
    Social Security number: _____
    Driver's license number: _____ Issuing state: _____
    Current residence address: _____
    Mailing address: _____
    Home telephone number: _____ Work phone: _____
    Name of employer: _____
    Address of employment: _____

Name of first child: _____
    Social Security number: _____
    Driver's license number: _____ Issuing state: _____
    Current residence address: _____
    Mailing address: _____
    Home telephone number: _____ Work phone: _____
    Name of employer: _____
    Address of employment: _____

Name of second child: _____
    Social Security number: _____
    Driver's license number: _____ Issuing state: _____
    Current residence address: _____
    Mailing address: _____
    Home telephone number: _____ Work phone: _____
    Name of employer: _____
    Address of employment: _____

Name of third child: _____
    Social Security number: _____
    Driver's license number: _____ Issuing state: _____
    Current residence address: _____
    Mailing address: _____
    Home telephone number: _____ Work phone: _____
    Name of employer: _____
    Address of employment: _____

Name of fourth child: _____
    Social Security number: _____
    Driver's license number: _____ Issuing state: _____
    Current residence address: _____
    Mailing address: _____
    Home telephone number: _____ Work phone: _____
    Name of employer: _____
    Address of employment: _____

Name of fifth child: _____
    Social Security number: _____
    Driver's license number: _____ Issuing state: _____
    Current residence address: _____
    Mailing address: _____
    Home telephone number: _____ Work phone: _____
    Name of employer: _____
    Address of employment: _____

Name of sixth child: _____
    Social Security number: _____
    Driver's license number: _____ Issuing state: _____
    Current residence address: _____
    Mailing address: _____
    Home telephone number: _____ Work phone: _____
    Name of employer: _____
    Address of employment: _____

Exhibit ___. Orders Re Property and Debts

A. SEPARATE PROPERTY CONFIRMED

☐ **1. Separate Property Confirmed to Petitioner**

THE COURT FINDS that certain property was and is the separate property of the Petitioner, and THE COURT ORDERS that the following property is confirmed as Petitioner's sole and separate property:

☐ **2. Separate Property Confirmed to Respondent**

THE COURT FINDS that certain property was and is the separate property of the Respondent, and THE COURT ORDERS that the following property is confirmed as Respondent's sole and separate property:

B. DIVISION OF COMMUNITY PROPERTY AND DEBTS

THE COURT ORDERS that the community property of the parties is divided as follows:

☐ **1. Court to Retain Jurisdiction Over Employee Retirement Benefits**

THE COURT FINDS that _____ is a participant in a retirement program known as _____

_____,
as to which the Court reserves jurisdiction to adjudicate the respective rights of the parties at a future date upon application of either party. THE COURT ORDERS that _____ shall not apply for or accept benefits under said program without prior written notice to the other party and application to this Court for determination and division of community rights in said plan. IT IS FURTHER ORDERED that any party requesting a division or clarification of retirement shall do so within two (2) years of the date this decree is signed by the court, or the party shall lose that right.

☐ **2. Petitioner's Property**

Petitioner is given the following as Petitioner's sole and separate property, and Respondent has no right, title, interest, or claim in and to such property:

2a. All property in Petitioner's care, custody or control or in Petitioner's name, and not otherwise specifically awarded to Respondent.

2b. ☐ The following specific property:

2c. ☐ A house or other real estate:

THE COURT ORDERS that Petitioner is awarded the following property as Petitioner's sole and separate property, and Respondent conveys to Petitioner all of Respondent's interest in such property, and Respondent is divested of all right, title, interest and claim and in and to that property:

[Street address and legal description of real property, including name of county and state.]

2d. ☐ The following retirement savings accounts (401k, IRA, SEP, etc.) in Petitioner's sole name:

2e. ☐ All cash in Petitioner's possession and all money on account in banks, savings institutions, or other financial institutions in Petitioner's sole name.

[This means you must separate your accounts **before** the judge signs the Decree]

2f. ☐ The following cars, trucks, or motorcycles: [List year, make and model.]

2g. ☐ Any and all policies of life insurance (including cash values) insuring the life of Petitioner.

2h. ☐ Additional property that Petitioner will keep:

☐ 3. Petitioner's Debts

THE COURT ORDERS that Petitioner pay the following community debts:

3a. ☐ All encumbrances, taxes, liens, assessments, or other charges due or to become due on real and personal property awarded to Petitioner in this decree unless express provision is made herein to the contrary.

3b. ☐ Balances due on mortgages secured by land and buildings awarded to the Petitioner in this decree.

3c. ☐ Community debts charged by Petitioner since _____, 20___, which the court finds to be the date of separation.

3d. ☐ Balances due on loans secured by vehicles awarded to Petitioner.

3e. Any debts solely in Petitioner's name, except as otherwise provided for herein.

3f. ☐ The following debts, charges, liabilities, and obligations that are not solely in Petitioner's name: [credit cards, student loans, medical bills, income taxes, etc.]

☐ 4. Respondent's Property

Respondent is given the following as Petitioner's sole and separate property, and Petitioner has no right, title, interest, or claim in and to such property:

4a. All property in Respondent's care, custody or control or in Respondent's name, and not otherwise specifically awarded to Petitioner.

4b. ☐ The following specific property:

4c. ☐ A house or other real estate:
THE COURT ORDERS that Respondent is awarded the following property as Respondent's sole and separate property, and Petitioner conveys to Respondent all of Petitioner's interest in such property, and Petitioner is divested of all right, title, interest and claim and in and to that property:
[Street address and legal description of real property, including name of county and state.]

4d. ☐ The following retirement savings accounts (401k, IRA, SEP, etc.) in Respondent's sole name:

4e. ☐ All cash in Respondent's possession and all money on account in banks, savings institutions, or other financial institutions in Respondent's sole name. [This means you must separate your accounts **before** the judge signs the Decree]

4f. ☐ The following cars, trucks, or motorcycles: [List year, make and model.]

4g. ☐ Any and all policies of life insurance (including cash values) insuring the life of Respondent.

4h. ☐ Additional property that Respondent will keep:

☐ **5. Respondent's Debts**

THE COURT ORDERS that Respondent pay the following community debts:

5a. ☐ All encumbrances, taxes, liens, assessments, or other charges due or to become due on real and personal property awarded to Respondent in this decree unless express provision is made herein to the contrary.

5b. ☐ Balances due on mortgages secured by land and buildings awarded to the Respondent in this decree.

5c. ☐ Community debts charged by Respondent since _____, 20___, which the court finds to be the date of separation.

5d. ☐ Balances due on loans secured by vehicles awarded to Respondent.

5e. Any debts solely in Respondent's name, except as otherwise provided for herein.

5f. ☐ The following debts, charges, liabilities, and obligations that are not solely in Respondent's name: [credit cards, student loans, medical bills, income taxes, etc.]

INFORMATION ON SUIT AFFECTING THE FAMILY RELATIONSHIP
(EXCLUDING ADOPTIONS)

SECTION I GENERAL INFORMATION (REQUIRED)	STATE FILE NUMBER

1a. COUNTY _____   1b. COURT NO. _____

1c. CAUSE NO. _____   1d. DATE OF ORDER (mm/dd/yyyy) _____

2. HAS THERE BEEN A FINDING BY THE COURT OF: ☐ DOMESTIC VIOLENCE?   ☐ CHILD ABUSE?

3. TYPE OF ORDER (CHECK ALL THAT APPLY):

☐ DIVORCE/ANNULMENT WITH CHILDREN(Sec. 1,2,3,4)   ☐ DIVORCE/ANNULMENT WITHOUT CHILDREN(Sec 1,2)

☐ PATERNITY WITH CHILD SUPPORT(Sec 1,3,4,5)   ☐ PATERNITY WITHOUT CHILD SUPPORT(Sec 1,3,5)

☐ CHILD SUPPORT OBLIGATION/MODIFICATION(Sec 1,3,4)   ☐ TERMINATION OF RIGHTS (Sec 1,3,6)

☐ CONSERVATORSHIP (Sec 1, 3)   ☐ OTHER (Specify) _____

☐ TRANSFER TO (Sec 1, 3) COUNTY _____ COURT NO. _____ STATE COURT ID# _____

4a. NAME OF ATTORNEY FOR PETITIONER	4b. ATTORNEY GENERAL ACCT/CASE #
4c. CURRENT MAILING ADDRESS STREET & NO. CITY STATE ZIP	4d. TELEPHONE NUMBER (including area code) ( )

SECTION 2 (IF APPLICABLE) REPORT OF DIVORCE OR ANNULMENT OF MARRIAGE		

	5. FIRST NAME MIDDLE LAST SUFFIX		6. DATE OF BIRTH (mm/dd/yyyy)
HUSBAND	7. PLACE OF BIRTH CITY STATE OR FOREIGN COUNTRY	8. RACE	9. SOCIAL SECURITY NUMBER
	10. USUAL RESIDENCE STREET NAME & NUMBER	CITY STATE	ZIP
WIFE	11. FIRST NAME MIDDLE LAST	MAIDEN	12. DATE OF BIRTH (mm/dd/yyyy)
	13. PLACE OF BIRTH CITY STATE OR FOREIGN COUNTRY	14. RACE	15. SOCIAL SECURITY NUMBER
	16. USUAL RESIDENCE STREET NAME & NUMBER CITY STATE ZIP		

17. NUMBER OF MINOR CHILDREN	18. DATE OF MARRIAGE (mm/dd/yyyy)	19. PLACE OF MARRIAGE City State	20. PETITIONER IS ☐ HUSBAND ☐ WIFE

SECTION 3 (IF APPLICABLE) CHILDREN AFFECTED BY THIS SUIT		

	21a. FIRST NAME MIDDLE LAST SUFFIX		21b. DATE OF BIRTH (mm/dd/yyyy)
CHILD 1	21c. SOCIAL SECURITY NUMBER	21d. SEX	21e. BIRTHPLACE CITY COUNTY STATE
	21f. PRIOR NAME OF CHILD: FIRST MIDDLE LAST SUFFIX	21g. NEW NAME OF CHILD FIRST MIDDLE LAST SUFFIX	
	22a. FIRST NAME MIDDLE LAST SUFFIX		22b. DATE OF BIRTH (mm/dd/yyyy)
CHILD 2	22c. SOCIAL SECURITY NUMBER	22d. SEX	22e. BIRTHPLACE CITY COUNTY STATE
	22f. PRIOR NAME OF CHILD: FIRST MIDDLE LAST SUFFIX	22g. NEW NAME OF CHILD FIRST MIDDLE LAST SUFFIX	
	23a. FIRST NAME MIDDLE LAST SUFFIX		23b. DATE OF BIRTH (mm/dd/yyyy)
CHILD 3	23c. SOCIAL SECURITY NUMBER	23d. SEX	23e. BIRTHPLACE CITY COUNTY STATE
	23f. PRIOR NAME OF CHILD FIRST MIDDLE LAST SUFFIX	23g. NEW NAME OF CHILD FIRST MIDDLE LAST SUFFIX	
	24a. FIRST NAME MIDDLE LAST SUFFIX		24b. DATE OF BIRTH (mm/dd/yyyy)
CHILD 4	24c. SOCIAL SECURITY NUMBER	24d. SEX	24e BIRTH CITY COUNTY STATE
	24f. PRIOR NAME OF CHILD FIRST MIDDLE LAST SUFFIX	24g. NEW NAME OF CHILD FIRST MIDDLE LAST SUFFIX	

1

SECTION 4 (IF APPLICABLE) OBLIGEE/OBLIGOR INFORMATION

OBLIGEE

THIS PARTY TO THE SUIT IS (CHECK ONE) ☐ 25a. TDPRS   ☐ 25b. NON-PARENT CONSERVATOR – COMPLETE 26 – 32

☐ 25c. HUSBAND AS SHOWN ON FRONT OF THIS FORM – COMPLETE 31 – 32 ONLY   ☐ 25d. WIFE AS SHOWN ON FRONT OF THIS FORM – COMPLETE 31 – 32 ONLY

☐ 25e. BIOLOGICAL FATHER – COMPLETE 26 – 32   ☐ 25f. BIOLOGICAL MOTHER – COMPLETE 26 – 32

26. FIRST NAME MIDDLE LAST SUFFIX	MAIDEN

27. DATE OF BIRTH (mm/dd/yyyy) | 28. PLACE OF BIRTH CITY STATE OR FOREIGN COUNTRY

29. USUAL RESIDENCE STREET NAME & NUMBER CITY COUNTY STATE ZIP

30. SOCIAL SECURITY NUMBER | 31. DRIVER LICENSE NO & STATE | 32. TELEPHONE NUMBER (   )

OBLIGOR #1

THIS PARTY TO THE SUIT IS (CHECK ONE)   ☐ 33a. NON-PARENT CONSERVATOR – COMPLETE 34 – 43

☐ 33b. HUSBAND AS SHOWN ON FRONT OF THIS FORM – COMPLETE 39 – 43 ONLY   ☐ 33c. WIFE AS SHOWN ON FRONT OF THIS FORM – COMPLETE 39 – 43 ONLY

☐ 33d. BIOLOGICAL FATHER – COMPLETE 34 – 43   ☐ 33e. BIOLOGICAL MOTHER – COMPLETE 34 – 43

34. FIRST NAME MIDDLE LAST SUFFIX MAIDEN

35. DATE OF BIRTH (mm/dd/yyyy) | 36. PLACE OF BIRTH CITY STATE OR FOREIGN COUNTRY

37. USUAL RESIDENCE STREET NAME & NUMBER CITY COUNTY STATE ZIP

38. SOCIAL SECURITY NUMBER | 39 DRIVER LICENSE NO. & STATE | 40. TELEPHONE NUMBER (   )

41. EMPLOYER NAME | 42. EMPLOYER TELEPHONE NUMBER

43. EMPLOYER PAYROLL ADDRESS STREET NAME & NUMBER CITY STATE ZIP

OBLIGOR #2

THIS PARTY TO THE SUIT IS (CHECK ONE)   ☐ 44a. NON-PARENT CONSERVATOR – COMPLETE 45 – 54

☐ 44b. HUSBAND AS SHOWN ON FRONT OF THIS FORM – COMPLETE 50 – 54 ONLY   ☐ 44c. WIFE AS SHOWN ON FRONT OF THIS FORM – COMPLETE 45 – 54 ONLY

☐ 44d. BIOLOGICAL FATHER – COMPLETE 45 – 54   ☐ 44e. BIOLOGICAL MOTHER – COMPLETE 45 – 54

45. FIRST NAME MIDDLE LAST SUFFIX MAIDEN

46. DATE OF BIRTH (mm/dd/yyyy) | 47. PLACE OF BIRTH CITY STATE OR FOREIGN COUNTRY

48. USUAL RESIDENCE STREET NAME & NUMBER CITY COUNTY STATE ZIP

49. SOCIAL SECURITY NUMBER | 50. DRIVER LICENSE NO & STATE | 51. TELEPHONE NUMBER

52. EMPLOYER NAME | 53. EMPLOYER TELEPHONE NUMBER

54. EMPLOYER PAYROLL ADDRESS STREET NAME & NUMBER CITY STATE ZIP

SECTION 5 (IF APPLICABLE) FOR ORDERS CONCERNING PATERNITY ESTABLISHMENT OF BIOLOGICAL FATHER

55. BIOLOGICAL FATHER'S NAME FIRST MIDDLE LAST | 56. DATE OF BIRTH (mm/dd/yyyy)

57. SOCIAL SECURITY NUMBER | 58. CURRENT MAILING ADDRESS STREET NAME & NUMBER CITY STATE ZIP

59. DOES THIS ORDER REMOVE INFORMATION PERTAINING TO A FATHER FROM A CHILD'S CERTIFICATE OF BIRTH? ☐ NO   ☐ YES

SECTION 6 TERMINATION OF RIGHTS – INFORMATION RELATED TO THE INDIVIDUAL(S) WHOSE RIGHTS ARE BEING TERMINATED IN THIS SUIT.

60a. FIRST NAME MIDDLE NAME LAST NAME SUFFIX	60b. RELATIONSHIP
61a. FIRST NAME MIDDLE NAME LAST NAME SUUFIX	61b. RELATIONSHIP
62a. FIRST NAME MIDDLE NAME LAST NAME SUFFIX	62b. RELATIONSHIP

COMMENTS: _____

_____

I CERTIFY THAT THE ABOVE ORDER WAS GRANTED ON THE
DATE AND PLACE AS STATED.

_____
SIGNATURE OF THE CLERK OF THE COURT

CAUSE NO. _____

IN THE MATTER OF THE MARRIAGE OF

_____ §

Petitioner [Print your full name]

AND

_____ §

Respondent [Print your spouse's full name]

AND IN THE INTEREST OF

MINOR CHILDREN:

_____ §

_____ §

_____ §

_____ §

_____ §

_____ §

[Print the full names of your children]

IN THE DISTRICT COURT OF

COUNTY, TEXAS

#_____ JUDICIAL DISTRICT

EMPLOYER'S ORDER TO WITHHOLD FROM EARNINGS FOR CHILD SUPPORT

The Court ORDERS you, the employer of _____, Obligor, to withhold income from the Obligor's disposable earnings from this employment as follows:

OBLIGOR: *(the person who pays child support)*

Name: _____ Social security Number _____

Address: _____

OBLIGEE: *(the person who receives child support)*

Name: _____ Social security Number _____

Address: _____

CHILDREN:

1. Child's name _____

Date of Birth: _____ Social Security #: _____

Date child turns 18 _____ Place of Birth: _____

2. Child's name _____

Date of Birth: _____ Social Security #: _____

Date child turns 18 _____ Place of Birth: _____

3. Child's name _____

Date of Birth: _____ Social Security #: _____

Date child turns 18 _____ Place of Birth: _____

4. Child's name _____

Date of Birth: _____ Social Security #: _____

Date child turns 18 _____ Place of Birth: _____

5. Child's name _____

Date of Birth: _____ Social Security #: _____

Date child turns 18 _____ Place of Birth: _____

6. Child's name _____

Date of Birth: _____ Social Security #: _____

Date child turns 18 _____ Place of Birth: _____

REFERENCE TO THE INCOME WITHHOLDING LAW.

Attached to this order is a copy of subchapter C, Chapter 158, of the Texas Family Code, which sets forth rights, duties, and potential liabilities of employers, in addition to the provisions of this order.

WITHHOLDING EARNINGS FOR CHILD SUPPORT.

The Court ORDERS that any employer of Obligor shall begin withholding from Obligor's disposable earnings no later than the first pay period following the date this order is served on that employer.

METHOD OF PAYMENT.

The Court ORDERS the employer, on each pay date, to remit all amounts withheld through the Texas Child Support State Disbursement Unit, P.O. Box 659791, San Antonio, Texas 78265-9791, for distribution according to law. The Court ORDERS the employer to include the following information with each payment:

1. The date of withholding,

2. The number assigned by the title IV-D agency (if available), the county identification number (if available) or the cause number: _____ ,

3. Obligor's Name [person who pays]: _____ , and

4. Obligee's Name [person who receives]: _____ .

MAXIMUM AMOUNT WITHHELD.

The maximum amount to be withheld shall not exceed 50 percent of Obligor's disposable earnings.

ORDER TO WITHHOLD.

The Court ORDERS the employer to withhold the following amounts from the earnings of Obligor:

If Obligor is PAID MONTHLY, which is:

$_____

$_____ on current support, and

$_____ on the medical support owed

(if the Obligor is reimbursing the Receiver for health insurance premiums for the children, and the reimbursement is included in the monthly child support amount.)

If Obligor is PAID TWICE MONTHLY, divide monthly child support amount by two, which is:

$_____

$_____ on current support, and

$_____ on the medical support owed.

If Obligor is PAID EVERY OTHER WEEK, multiply monthly child support by 12, then divide by 26, which is:

$_____

$_____ on current support, and

$_____ on the medical support owed.

If Obligor is PAID EVERY WEEK, multiply monthly child support by 12, then divide by 5, which is:

$_____

$_____ on current support, and

$_____ on the medical support owed.

Until one of the following events has occurred with respect to each and every subject child:
1. The child reaches the age of eighteen years, *provided that,*
   (a) The child is enrolled in an accredited secondary school program leading toward a high school diploma, or in courses for joint high school and junior college credit, or on a full-time basis in a private secondary school program leading toward a high school diploma; and
   (b) The child is complying with the minimum attendance requirements of Chapter 25 of the Education Code, or the minimum attendance requirements imposed by the school in which the child is enrolled, if the child is enrolled in a private secondary school;
   then the periodic child-support payments shall continue to be due and paid until the end of the month in which the child graduates; or
2. The child marries; or commences active service in the United States military forces; or
3. The child dies; or
4. The child's disabilities are otherwise removed for general purposes; or
5. The date on which the Court enters a further order modifying child support, or
6. The Court makes a finding that the child is 18 years of age or older and has failed to comply with the enrollment or attendance requirements described above; or
7. The marriage or re-marriage of Obligor and Obligee to each other; or
8. Further order amending or terminating this order.

If more than one child is the subject of this Order to Withhold Earnings for Child Support, then the amount of support to be withheld shall be as stated above until the first occurrence of one of the events stated above for one of the children.

Thereafter, Obligor is ORDERED to pay to Obligee child support of _____ per month, due and payable on the first day of the first month immediately following the date of the earliest occurrence of one of the events specified above for another child and the same amount being due on the first day of each month thereafter until the next occurrence of one of the events specified above for another child.

Thereafter, Obligor is ORDERED to pay to Obligee child support of _____ per month, due and payable on the first day of the first month immediately following the date of the earliest occurrence of one of the events specified above for another child and the same amount being due on the first day of each month thereafter until the next occurrence of one of the events specified above for another child.

Thereafter, Obligor is ORDERED to pay to Obligee child support of _____ per month, due and payable on the first day of the first month immediately following the date of the earliest occurrence of one of the events specified above for another child and the same amount being due on the first day of each month thereafter until the next occurrence of one of the events specified above for another child.

Thereafter, Obligor is ORDERED to pay to Obligee child support of _____ per month, due and payable on the first day of the first month immediately following the date of the earliest occurrence of one of the events specified above for another child and the same amount being due on the first day of each month thereafter until the next occurrence of one of the events specified above for another child.

Thereafter, Obligor is ORDERED to pay to Obligee child support of _____ per month, due and payable on the first day of the first month immediately following the date of the earliest occurrence of one of the events specified above for another child and the same amount being due on the first day of each month thereafter until the next occurrence of one of the events specified above for another child.

CALCULATING DISPOSABLE EARNINGS.

The employer shall calculate Obligor's disposable earnings, which are subject to withholding for child support, as follows:

    A. Determine the "earnings" of Obligor. "Earnings" means a payment to or due an individual, regardless of source and how denominated, and includes a periodic or lump-sum payment for wages, salary, compensation received as an independent contractor, overtime pay, severance pay, commission, bonus, and interest income; payments made under a pension, an annuity, workers' compensation, and a disability or retirement program; and unemployment benefits.

    B. Subtract the following sums to calculate Obligor's "disposable earnings:"

        (1) Any amounts required by law to be withheld, that is, federal income tax and federal FICA or OASI tax (Social Security), Railroad Retirement Act contributions;

        (2) Union dues;

        (3) Nondiscretionary retirement contributions by the Obligor; and

        (4) Medical, hospitalization, and disability insurance coverage for Obligor and Obligor's children.

MORE THAN ONE ORDER WITHHOLDING.

If you receive more than one "Writ of Withholding" or "Employer's Order to Withhold Earnings for Child Support" for Obligor, you shall pay an equal amount towards the current support portion of all orders or writs until each is individually complied with, and thereafter pay equal amounts on the arrearage portion of all orders or writs until each is complied with, or until the maximum total amount of allowable withholding, 50 percent of the Obligor's disposable earnings, is reached, whichever occurs first.

TERMINATION OF WITHHOLDING.

For as long as Obligor is employed by you, the employer of Obligor, you shall continue to withhold income in accordance with this order until the youngest child reaches eighteen years of age or graduates from high school, whichever occurs last. This order indicates when each child reaches eighteen years of age. Written notice from a child's school of the child's high-school graduation will constitute notice of graduation to you.

NOTICE OF CHANGE OF EMPLOYMENT.

The Court ORDERS the employer to notify the Court and Obligee within seven days of the date that Obligor terminates employment. The Court ORDERS the employer to provide Obligor's last known address and the name and address of the Obligor's new employer, if known.

MEDICAL CHILD-SUPPORT ORDER

☐ If this box is checked, the Court ORDERS the employer to provide health insurance for Obligor's children as set out in the Medical Child-Support Order, a copy of which is attached to this order and incorporated in it for all purposes.

SIGNED on _____ by _____, JUDGE PRESIDING

Cause Number _____

IN THE MATTER OF THE MARRIAGE OF: IN THE DISTRICT COURT

_____, Petitioner

    ____ JUDICIAL DISTRICT

AND

_____, Respondent   _____ COUNTY, TEXAS

EMPLOYER'S ORDER TO WITHHOLD
EARNINGS FOR SPOUSAL MAINTENANCE

The Court ORDERS you, the employer of OBLIGOR, to withhold income from his/her disposable earnings from this employment as follows:

Obligor:

    Name: _____

    Address:_____

    Social Security number: _____

Obligee:

    Name: _____

    Address: _____

    Social Security number: _____

Withholding from Earnings for Spousal Maintenance

The Court ORDERS that any employer of OBLIGOR shall begin withholding from his/her disposable earnings no later than the first pay period following the date this order is served on that employer.

Method of Payment

The Court ORDERS the employer to pay all amounts withheld on each payday to OBLIGEE at the address stated above, or at any address provided to you by OBLIGEE in writing.

Order to Withhold

The Court ORDERS employer to withhold the following amounts from the earnings of OBLIGOR:

(1) $_____ on current spousal maintenance, if OBLIGOR is paid monthly:

(2) $_____ on current spousal maintenance, if OBLIGOR is paid twice monthly:

(3) $_____ on current spousal maintenance, if OBLIGOR is paid every other week:

(4) $_____ on current spousal maintenance, if OBLIGOR is paid every week:

The Court ORDERS the employer to withhold the above amount until: _____

Calculating Disposable Earnings

The employer shall calculate OBLIGOR's disposable earnings, which are subject to withholding for child support, as follows:

1. Determine the "earnings" of OBLIGOR, which means compensation paid or payable for personal services, whether called wages, salary, compensation received as an independent contractor, overtime pay, severance pay, commission, bonus, or otherwise, including periodic payments pursuant to a pension, an annuity, workers' compensation, a disability and retirement program, and unemployment benefits;

2. Subtract the following sums to calculate OBLIGOR's "disposable earnings":
   a. any amounts required by law to be withheld, that is, federal income tax and federal FICA or OASI tax (Social Security) and Railroad Retirement Act contributions;
   b. union dues;
   c. nondiscretionary retirement contributions by OBLIGOR; and
   d. medical, hospitalization, and disability insurance coverage for OBLIGOR and OBLIGOR's children.

Notice of Change of Employment

The Court ORDERS the employer to notify the Court and OBLIGEE within seven days of the date that OBLIGOR terminates employment. The Court ORDERS the employer to provide OBLIGOR's last known address and the name and address of his new employer, if known.

Signed on _____

_____
Judge Presiding

Cause Number _____

IN THE MATTER OF THE MARRIAGE OF: **IN THE DISTRICT COURT**

_____, **Petitioner**

AND   ____ **JUDICIAL DISTRICT**

_____, **Respondent**   _____ **COUNTY, TEXAS**

AND IN THE INTEREST OF _____

_____ **MINOR CHILD(REN)**

REQUEST TO ISSUE
EMPLOYER'S ORDER TO WITHHOLD
EARNINGS FOR CHILD SUPPORT OR SPOUSAL MAINTENANCE

To the Clerk of the Court:

Please issue a certified copy of the following order in this cause:

☐ Order/Notice to Withhold from Earnings for Child Support,
   signed by the Court on _____ .

☐ Employer's Order to Withholding Earnings for Spousal Maintenance,
   signed by the Court on _____ .

And deliver the order to:

Obligor's/Payor's Employer: _____

Address: _____

City, State, Zip: _____

Submitted on _____

_____
Obligee/Payee

_____
Address

Cause Number _____

IN THE MATTER OF THE MARRIAGE OF: IN THE DISTRICT COURT

_____, Petitioner

AND   ____ JUDICIAL DISTRICT

_____, Respondent   _____ COUNTY, TEXAS

SERVICEMEMBERS CIVIL RELIEF ACT AFFIDAVIT

Affiant, being duly sworn on his/her oath deposes and says under penalty of perjury that:

I am ☐ Petitioner ☐ Petitioner's agent in the above entitled matter.

I have ☐ personal knowledge that Respondent is not in the military on active duty.
☐ made a personal investigation of records of the United States military.
☐ researched the following internet military site _____
to discover whether Respondent is in the military.
☐ researched whether Respondent is in the military from the following sources:

_____

Based upon the foregoing, it is my belief that

☐ the above-named Respondent is **not** in the military service on active duty.
☐ the above-named Respondent is in the military service on active duty.
☐ I have been unable to determine whether or not the defendant is in the military service on active duty.

I understand that statements in this document are made under penalty of perjury and that making a false statement is a violation of Federal Law and is subject to both fine and imprisonment.

_____
                                            Affiant

Subscribed and sworn to before me this _____ Day of _____, 20___

_____
Notary public in and for the state of Texas
or Officer Authorized to Administer Oaths
or Clerk of the Court   (strike all but one)

Cause Number _____

IN THE MATTER OF THE MARRIAGE OF: IN THE DISTRICT COURT

_____, Petitioner

                                                 ____ JUDICIAL DISTRICT
AND

_____, Respondent   _____ COUNTY, TEXAS

AND IN THE INTEREST OF _____

_____ MINOR CHILD(REN)

FINANCIAL INFORMATION AND PROPOSED SUPPORT DECISION

I, _____, would testify under oath in open Court that the following information is true and correct. I understand that at a Court hearing I may be required to prove these amounts by testimony and by records such as pay vouchers, canceled checks, receipts and bills.

A. Petitioner's monthly resources (Describe each source)	Gross Amount	Allowed deductions (Soc.Sec., union dues, w/holding tax, health insurance for child)
1. _____	$_____	$_____
2. _____	$_____	$_____
3. _____	$_____	$_____
4. _____	$_____	$_____
Total Resources Each Month	$_____	$_____

B. Respondent's monthly resources (Describe each source)	Gross Amount	Allowed deductions (Soc. Sec., union dues, w/holding tax, health insurance for child)
1. _____	$_____	$_____
2. _____	$_____	$_____
3. _____	$_____	$_____
4. _____	$_____	$_____
Total Resources Each Month	$_____	$_____

C. Total money needed per month by custodial parent and minor child(ren)
(amounts not paid monthly are averages)

1. Rent or house payment	$_____	16. Clothing & shoes	$_____
2. Property tax not included in item 1	$_____	17. Insurance - auto	$_____
		18. Insurance - life	$_____
3. Residence maintenance	$_____	19. Insurance - health	$_____
4. Home insurance	$_____	20. Child care	$_____
5. Utilities	$_____	21. Child activities	$_____
6. Telephone (avg./mo.)	$_____	22. Cable TV, newspaper	$_____
7. Groceries & supplies	$_____	23. Other:_____	$_____
8. Meals away from home	$_____	_____	$_____
9. School lunches	$_____	_____	$_____
10. Dental	$_____	_____	$_____
11. Medical & medicine	$_____	_____	$_____
12. Laundry, dry clean	$_____	24. Support or alimony payments to others	$_____
13. Gas & car maintenance	$_____		
14. Entertainment	$_____	25. Monthly debt payments (total of item D)	$_____
15. Haircuts	$_____		

Total Needed Per Month (Total of items C 1-25) $_____

Difference Between Money Received & Money Needed $_____

D. Monthly Payments On Indebtedness

Description Of Debt	Balance Owed	Amount Of Monthly Pmt.	Date Of Final Pmt.
1._____	$_____	$_____	_____
2._____	$_____	$_____	_____
3._____	$_____	$_____	_____
4._____	$_____	$_____	_____
5._____	$_____	$_____	_____
6._____	$_____	$_____	_____

Total Monthly Payments $_____
(enter on line C25 above)

I intend to ask the Court to set support at $_____ per month.

Signed this____ day of _____, 20___

_____
Petitioner, Pro Se

Cause Number _____

IN THE MATTER OF THE MARRIAGE OF: **IN THE DISTRICT COURT**

_____, Petitioner

AND   ____ **JUDICIAL DISTRICT**

_____, Respondent   _____ **COUNTY, TEXAS**

AND IN THE INTEREST OF _____

_____ **MINOR CHILD(REN)**

AFFIDAVIT OF INABILITY TO PAY

THE STATE OF TEXAS
COUNTY OF _____

BEFORE ME, the undersigned authority, on this day personally appeared
_____, who being by me duly sworn, on oath stated:

My name is _____. I am the Petitioner in the above referenced case. I believe that I have a meritorious claim. I verify that the statements made in this claim are true and correct.

I am unable to pay court costs for the following reasons.

I have approximately $_____ in monthly expenses.

I have debts of approximately $_____.

☐ I own no real estate, stocks, bonds or other property
    other than _____.

☐ I currently have only $ _____ in cash.

☐ I am unemployed.

☐ My monthly income consists of $_____ from the following sources

_____.

_____.

☐ I have no other income.

☐ I do not have access to any income from my spouse.

Signed: _____
                                    Plaintiff

SUBSCRIBED AND SWORN TO BEFORE ME
on this _____ day of _____, 20___.

_____
                Notary Public, State of Texas
        or Officer Authorized to Administer Oaths

STATE OF TEXAS
COUNTY OF _____

POWER OF ATTORNEY TO TRANSFER MOTOR VEHICLE

I, _____, of the state and county named above, for good and valuable consideration constitute and appoint _____, of _____ (city, county, state) my agent and attorney in fact, in my name, place, and stead, to convey and transfer all of my right, title and interest in one _____ (year, make, model) motor vehicle, vehicle identification number _____, to whomever s/he may desire and to execute, in my name as attorney in fact, any and all instruments necessary for such conveyance and transfer.

SIGNED on _____, 20___.

_____

ACKNOWLEDGEMENT

STATE OF TEXAS
COUNTY OF _____

This instrument was acknowledged before me on
_____, 20__, by _____

_____
Notary Public, State of Texas
or Officer Authorized to Administer Oaths

SPECIAL WARRANTY DEED

Grantor's name _____

of _____ County, Texas ("Grantor") for and in consideration of:

The sum of TEN DOLLARS AND NO CENTS ($10.00) and other good and valuable consideration, namely the division of property in:

Cause No. _____, styled: "In the Matter of the Marriage of

_____ and _____"

_____ Judicial District Court of _____ County, Texas

does GRANT, SELL and CONVEY to

Grantee's Name _____

of _____ County, Texas, ("Grantee"), Grantee's heirs, executors, administrators, successors or assigns, the following described real property:

Including assignments of the casualty insurance policy on the property and all escrow funds for payment of taxes and insurance premiums, to have and to hold, together with all and singular the rights and appurtenances thereto in anywise belonging forever. Grantor hereby binds Grantor, Grantor's heirs, executors, administrators, successors or assigns, to warrant and defend forever all and singular the property to Grantee, and Grantee's heirs, executors, administrators, successors or assigns against every person claiming lawfully or to claim the same or any part thereof, except as to any reservations, valid restrictions, easements, rights of way, maintenance charges, together with any lien securing the maintenance charges, zoning laws, ordinances of municipal or other governmental agencies or authorities, and conditions and covenants, if any, if applicable to and enforceable against the property described above of record when the claim is by, through or under Grantor, but not otherwise. Grantee assumes all ad valorem taxes due on the property for the current year.

EXECUTED THIS ___ day of _____, 20___, at _____ County, Texas.

_____
GRANTOR

STATE OF TEXAS   }
COUNTY OF _____   }

This instrument was acknowledged before me on the ___ day of _____, 20___ by _____.

_____
NOTARY PUBLIC, STATE OF TEXAS

AFTER RECORDING RETURN TO GRANTEE AT: